PATRICK HAMILTON

His Life and Work:
A Critical Study

John Harding

GREENWICH EXCHANGE
LONDON

Greenwich Exchange, London

Patrick Hamilton
His Life and Work: A Critical Study
© John Harding 2007

First published in Great Britain in 2007
All rights reserved

This book is sold subject to the conditions that it shall not, by way of trade or otherwise, be lent, resold, hired out, or otherwise circulated without the publisher's prior consent in any form of binding or cover other than that in which it is published and without a similar condition including this condition being imposed on the subsequent publisher.

Printed and bound by Q3 Digital/Litho, Loughborough
Tel: 01509 213456
Typesetting and layout by Albion Associates, London
Tel: 020 8852 4646
Cover design by December Publications, Belfast
Tel: 028 90286559

Cover: © National Portrait Gallery

Greenwich Exchange Website: www.greenex.co.uk

Cataloguing in Publication Data is available from the British Library

ISBN-13: 978-1-871551-99-0
ISBN-10: 1-871551-99-4

Acknowledgements

Surprisingly, there are no books devoted to the life and work of Patrick Hamilton currently in print. In writing this short study, I have had to rely heavily on a number of earlier sources. For the biographical sections, I have drawn on two excellent biographies written in the early 1990s by Nigel Jones and Sean French. These standard works have been out of print for far too long and deserve to be re-issued as Hamilton's star waxes bright once again.

There has, inevitably, been a certain amount of academic interest in Hamilton, particularly from left-leaning writers or those concerned specifically with the politics of Hamilton's fiction. Professor Peter Widdowson of the University of Gloucestershire, and a long-time fan of Hamilton's, oversaw the re-issue of Hamilton's 'lost' socialist critique of Britain, *Impromptu in Moribundia*, in 1999 and has written some penetrating pieces on his œuvre. Neil Maycroft wrote an interesting analysis of the same book in 2004, while Dr Brian McKenna produced a fascinating critique of *Moribundia* in 1999. Students interested in taking their study of Hamilton further would do well to start with these important articles. I have only been able to touch briefly on their conclusions. Brian McKenna's work on Hamilton is the most extensive. His doctoral thesis on Hamilton, as well as pieces on Hamilton's alcohol addiction, are essential reading for any serious study of Hamilton's work. Two other academic pieces are worthy of note: Professor Thierry Labica, of the University of Paris has written an intriguing article on conversation as a metaphor for warfare in Hamilton's novels. (He reveals, in passing, that another French academic, Prof Jean-Jacques Lecercle, sees in Hamilton a Marxist and alcoholic Jane Austen!); Simon Goulding, meanwhile, has looked closely at the location of Hamilton's *The Midnight Bell* in that area of London known as Fitzrovia, and his consideration of the public house space adds greatly to our understanding of Hamilton's closely observed world; Professor Phil Tew, meanwhile, has delved perceptively into the criminal mind of one of Hamilton's most intriguing characters, Gorse.

Hamilton has always been a 'writer's writer' and the re-issue of some of his greatest novels, not to mention the success of the TV adaptation of *Twenty Thousand Streets Under The Sky* has seen some entertaining pieces written by contemporary writers such as Dan Rhodes and Iain Sinclair, Laura Thomson and John Branston.

To all these writers, and many more, I would like to offer my thanks and appreciation.

Contents

Introduction: Contempories and Influences	ix
1 The Tyro Novelist	1
Craven House	8
2 Rush to Fame: London Laid Bare	14
Twenty Thousand Streets Under the Sky:	19
The Midnight Bell	20
The Siege of Pleasure	26
The Plains of Cement	28
3 Socialist Un-Realism: A Dystopian Journey	34
Impromptu in Moribunda	38
4 Finest Hours: The Home Front	44
Hangover Square	47
The Slaves of Solitude	57
5 Final Years: The Midnight Bell Tolls	64
The Gorse Trilogy:	66
The West Pier	67
Mr Stimpson and Mr Gorse	71
Unknown Assailant	75
6 Hamilton on Stage and Screen	79
Postscript: Be Always Drunken	87
References and Further Reading	91

Introduction: Contemporaries and Influences

Hamilton ... is a sort of urban Thomas Hardy. He is always a pleasure to read, and as social historian he is unparalleled.

Nick Hornby

Patrick Hamilton defies categorizing, being neither part of a 'movement' nor even a 'period'. He has, at times, been considered a Fitzrovian, as one of his most successful novels was set in a public house in the heart of that fabled London literary district. However, Julian MacLaren-Ross, the best and wittiest chronicler of that particular literary coterie, who frequently talked about Hamilton and was a keen admirer of his fiction, never actually met him.

Neither was Hamilton part of the Bloomsbury Set, something of a surprise considering his Marxist politics, the times he lived through and the places in which he resided. But whereas his contemporaries – the likes of Virginia Woolf, Vita Sackville-West, E.M. Forster, Lytton Strachey, Vanessa Bell – all became household names, it was Hamilton's work that became famous, rather than his name. He was, and remained for decades, a strangely 'invisible' writer – a dangerous situation where literary posterity is concerned.

In 1968 Doris Lessing wrote in *The Times*: "Patrick Hamilton was a marvellous novelist who's grossly neglected ... I'm continually amazed that there's a kind of roll call of OK names from the 1930s, sort of Auden, Isherwood, etc., but Hamilton is never on them and he's a much better writer than any of them ... [he] was very much outside the tradition of an upper-class or middle-class writer of that time."

Paradoxically, this may in part be due to Hamilton's amazing versatility. Uniquely, he excelled in two, maybe three distinct genres. How many writers of quality prose fiction have also been successful playwrights? What's more, his were not simply avant-garde plays performed before a select audience. They were internationally-acclaimed West End hits that continued to earn him vast sums of money throughout his life. Furthermore, he adapted these plays for live transmission on the embryonic television screen before the Second World War. As if that wasn't enough, he regularly produced highly original radio plays that captured audiences in their millions. Hamilton also had the privilege (or was it the misfortune?) to have seen at least three of his novels and plays reproduced on the silver screen.

Such ubiquity can be off-putting to those struggling to succeed in one particular area. There may also have been a suspicion, certainly amongst the aesthetic elite, that such wild success was somehow 'non-U'. He moved, perhaps, too easily between diverse, creative situations, to be true. He also had a practical, almost hard-nosed approach to the craft of writing that eschewed unnecessary theory and philosophising. His success in producing wildly successful stage drama was due to his close-hand study of what actually worked on a practical level. There was little mystery about it.

Where his 'image' was concerned, Hamilton made certain definite choices very early on. There was a time at the start of his career when he wondered if he ought to develop a public persona but was advised against it by his brother, Bruce – his closest literary confidant. Bruce was a writer whose work never approached Hamilton's but which, in many ways, mirrored it in theme and style and from which Hamilton often borrowed and adapted.

Not that Hamilton was averse to bright lights and good living. His stage connections – theatrical producers, actors, agents, etc. – were usually the ones to whom he gravitated when in search of a good time. And he certainly enjoyed a good time. Thus, he conspicuously failed to make connections with writers of his own age.

He was certainly praised by many of his contemporaries – Walter Allen, Graham Greene, Doris Lessing, Anthony Powell, Julian Symons amongst them – but only from a distance.

Thus, without the support of a contemporary literary group or clique that might have provided him with support, he came to rely instead on a group of male friends, all older than himself. They all belonged to an earlier generation of writers, men like W.W. Jacobs, Compton Mackenzie, Edward Marsh and Hugh Walpole. His closest literary friend and also his publisher, Michael Sadleir, had started a literary magazine with John Middleton Murry as far back as 1911 when Hamilton was only seven years old! Unfortunately, this unwillingness to consort with his contemporaries had unfortunate consequences late in his career. His 'old friends' had a conception of the novel that would differ radically from Hamilton's own disturbing, idiosyncratic comic gift. Their attacks on his final novels helped kill his creative spirit.

Hamilton had, however, plenty of opportunity to enter the wider literary world. On first acquaintance in 1926, Sadleir invited him to a PEN (Poets, Playwrights, Essayists and Novelists) dinner. This was a worldwide association of writers founded in 1921 to promote friendship and intellectual co-operation among writers everywhere. Its president was John Galsworthy, author of the recently published *Forsyte Saga* and the dinner provided Hamilton with a rare encounter with the avant-garde: James Joyce was the guest of honour and gave a little speech.

But Hamilton had little regard for Modernism and says as much in his novel *Impromptu in Moribundia*: "Eliot, Joyce, Huxley, Lawrence, Sitwell, Graves, Sassoon might seem rebels but they are for the most part hopelessly and morbidly turned in upon themselves and sterile in consequence". As for Bernard Shaw and H.G. Wells "there was nowhere any deep-seated change lurking behind the highly-readable polemics of these two and time would expose the unreality and irrelevance of their teachings".

There is no evidence that Hamilton went to another PEN dinner. He did join the Omar Khayyám Dining Society, and attended their annual banquets for years but this was hardly a literary hot-bed. Perversely, instead of joining the stage-oriented Garrick Club, he chose the Savile Club in New Bond Street. Here he found himself in the company of radio journalists from nearby Broadcasting House, filmmakers, television producers and scriptwriters. There simply was no pinning him down.

As for his acknowledged influences, according to Claud Cockburn, Charles Dickens was the author who exerted by far the most powerful purely literary influence on him. *Hard Times* was the book which impressed him most profoundly. Thomas Hardy and Joseph Conrad were also important to him. Hamilton once commented to his brother after reading Osbert Sitwell's novel *After the Bombardment* that it, along with Arnold Bennett's *The Old Wives Tales*, "are the only two novels (which I have read anyway) which really add up to anything in our time".

Today, his work attracts a cult following of distinguished fans, despite the fact that his books have been hard to come by. The biographer and keen Hamilton fan, Michael Holroyd, had never heard of him until, he says, "I found him myself by accident, in a public library, when I was a young man. I was browsing when I came across his book *Hangover Square*. I found out later that this was a great place to start. It is a thriller that really thrills, and after reading it, I was hooked". This led him on to *20,000 Streets* – and to concluding that Hamilton was an "undiscovered" genius.

Long-time contemporary admirers include Antonia Fraser, Nick Hornby, Keith Waterhouse, D.J. Taylor, Iain Sinclair and Lynn Truss. Interestingly, Keith Waterhouse, in his novel *Palace Pier* has conceived a novel within a novel in that his plot revolves around a supposedly undiscovered novel of Hamilton's from which Waterhouse quotes a number of pastiches. Peter Ackroyd, meanwhile, has judged Hamilton to be an important contributor to the tradition of the London novel and, along with Elizabeth Bowen, the most important exponent of the genre in the 1940s.

Doris Lessing perfectly sums up just why we should read Patrick Hamilton today: "He wrote novels about ordinary people. He wrote more sense about England and what was going on in England in the 1930s than anybody else I can think of, and his novels are true now. You can go into any pub and see it going on."

1

The Tyro Novelist

1904-1927 Childhood, youth, first success.
Craven House

Patrick Hamilton was born on 17th March 1904 in Hassocks, a prosperous village situated at the foot of the South Downs just north of Brighton on England's south coast. He was the youngest of three children born to parents who were both on their second marriages. His father, Bernard Hamilton, was a barrister who, during the course of Patrick's early childhood, managed to fritter away a considerable inheritance (£100,000 in 1884, at that time a veritable fortune) leading a life of self-indulgence and extravagance. He was also a snob and a self-dramatist, claiming the status of a war veteran (he never fought), a barrister (he never practised), as well as being of aristocratic lineage (his father was a rector). Intriguingly, he did manage to publish several historical novels of varying quality and on Patrick's birth certificate wrote "author" under the "Occupation of Father".

Bernard was described by biographer Michael Holroyd as, "a comedian equipped with a monocle but no sense of humour, a chameleon-like figure given to self-dramatisation, who nevertheless drank to be rid of himself."

Fortunately for Patrick and the rest of the family, Bernard spent much of his time away, either abroad or in London with various mistresses. Unfortunately, when he returned he was often drunk and resentful, hated and feared by his children, and barely tolerated by his wife. Although many of Bernard's personal traits – his extravagant and sometime idiotic use of language, in particular – would be used by Patrick in his fiction – Bernard himself would be a source of great personal and emotional anxiety to his youngest son. The latter's subsequent descent into destructive alcoholism would be an obvious consequence.

Bernard's first wife had been a prostitute who committed suicide by throwing herself under a train. His second, Patrick's mother, Ellen, had also been briefly married – to another womaniser whom she divorced almost as soon as she married him. She shared some of Bernard's less likeable characteristics. She was a snob and a heavy drinker but she also possessed certain minor talents such as playing the piano and copying old master paintings. Before Patrick's birth, she wrote some largely forgettable light fiction. (Her novel, *The Husband Hunter*, was later adapted for the silent screen in 1920.) However, with no money of her own, she remained tied to her unfaithful, abusive husband for her children's sake. That she was possessive to an unhealthy degree would cause all three children – Patrick in particular – further unhappiness.

From his earliest days, Patrick was intellectually curious, naturally asking frank questions about anything that puzzled him. He was thus something of an inconvenience to the various nurses deputed to look after him. As he later explained, he was

> well fed, cared for clothed, etc. – but that does not mean that there was any absence of anxieties and neuroses of all sorts, which were made more expressive, rather than disentangled, by various women with whom I spent most of my time – nannies.

He recalled a tendency to panic as a child: calling out to his nurse every ten minutes after the light went out for reassurance that she was still there somewhere as he couldn't bring himself to believe she was. He agonised over the simplest of things:

> They shouted that the toes were pigs – that one went to market, that one stayed at home, that one had roast beef, that one had none and that one went 'Wee-wee-wee-wee!' all the way home. But what was the 'market'? Why did one pig have roast beef and the other none? Where did the justice lie? Which pig gained? Could toes, in fact, be pigs? What's more the rhyme didn't scan nor did home rhyme with none.

Not surprisingly, his childhood was riddled with disappointments and disillusions. Christmas, with all its deceptive allure, was a particular letdown. He wrote: "The sense that once the gaudy wrappings were ripped off, life itself was a letdown, a cheat". This was to seep into him and gradually shaped his wary cynicism.

Nurses, he bemoaned, had a tendency to tease him with story-starts which they simply repeated over and over again. He recalled being kept on tenterhooks and invariably being disappointed when the tales failed to develop. Being a child with an incredibly retentive memory, a knack of storing up impressions of people and objects and possessing a keen awareness for emotional stress, he would employ the gut tension he felt at such times in later years when writing his popular stage plays.

Patrick's principal source of childhood solace and companionship would be his elder brother Bruce, who taught him to read, to ride a bike, and who shared his consuming interest in reading and telling 'made-up' stories. The two boys decided from a very early age that they would make literature their ambition and pledged themselves to literary success. It was a pact that would prove something of a burden for Bruce, who would always find himself overshadowed by his younger, more talented brother.

Patrick first aspired to be a poet and recalled having a juvenile preoccupation with Keats. Later in life he would tell a journalist, "While I lived the life of an ordinary boy, a poetic yearning developed by degrees until, all unconsciously as to how I reached that state of mind, I was sure that some day I was going to be a great poet."

The brothers' literary passions embraced the traditional 'canon': the lyrics of Wordsworth, Shelley, Tennyson, Milton, Spenser, etc., with little interest in contemporary fiction or poetry. As a teenager, Patrick wrote a long essay in verse called 'Modernism'. It was an assault on the Movement and an indictment of all those trends, chiefly in poetry but also in the whole field of contemporary creativity, that seemed to him to be leading away from simplicity and sincerity. It was a stance that would never alter. When he began publishing fiction, it would be work totally out of sync with the 'spirit of the age': T.S. Eliot, Ernest Hemingway, Virginia Woolf were all publishing seminal modernist tracts at this time but they might never have existed where Patrick was concerned. His models would be traditional novelists such as Compton Mackenzie and Alec Waugh.

In the early years of his life, before his father's money ran out, the family lived well. The first family home, Dale House, in Hassocks, was a substantial building with a beautiful garden requiring a staff of maids, governesses and gardeners. When he was four, they moved to another large, well-appointed house, this time in along the coast in Hove. But, despite the advantage of wealth, his formal education was irregular and incomplete.

Aged eight in 1912, Patrick entered Holland House School in Hove, but, two years later, soon after the First World War began, the family moved temporarily to Chiswick, West London, fearing a German coastal invasion. Here, in 1915, he was placed in a small preparatory school called Colet Court but when his brother Bruce fell ill their mother took them all back to Brighton. Patrick then chose to return to Colet Court as a boarder but was unhappy there and when tales of "fetid sexuality of dormitory life" reached his mother's ears via Bruce, he was promptly withdrawn, returning to Holland House as a boarder. In 1918 he entered Westminster School in London but, early in 1919, he was struck down by the worldwide flu epidemic and was withdrawn yet again, never to return. At 15 years of age, his formal education was over. Patrick never let this worry him – in fact, he became something of an autodidact, closely studying Friedrich Nietzsch and Karl Marx and accumulating his own extensive library.

Although school itself had not been a particularly unhappy or damaging experience, he'd been repelled (as well as morbidly fascinated) by what he considered the sheer idiocy of it all. The bullying, the routine, the boredom – all of these he would draw upon later in his novels. It would be the pre-pubescent, pre-sexual prep-school days that he would always portray for there was little else he knew about.

As a teenager, his social circle was constricted for the most part to his brother and sister. His relationship with his sister Lalla was close and would prove crucial for his future in a practical sense. Like her mother, Lalla had aspirations to be an actress and eventually obtained regular work in the theatre, acting under the name Diana Hamilton. She soon fell in love with an older, at that time unsuccessful, actor and playwright called Sutton Vane and they married in mid-1922.

By 1920, when Hamilton's father returned to the family home from army service with most of his fortune gone, straitened times beckoned. Sixteen-year-old Patrick was urged to enrol in a commercial college near Holborn, the intention being to go to University of London and get a degree. But, though his academic endeavours would soon fade, this short period of his life would affect his subsequent development as a novelist.

In order to escape the tensions and demands of family life now that his father was back home, he took lodgings at a small hotel, the White House, in Earls Court Square. Throughout his life, when under emotional pressure, Hamilton would retreat into similar guest-houses, furnished rooms or small hotels. They suited both his temperament and his writing habits. What's more, they would furnish him with valuable material for his novels. In such enclosed, somewhat stifling worlds he was able to observe at close hand people's behavioural 'tics', their speech patterns, their preoccupations. Guest houses and public houses would be essential settings for much of his finest fiction.

It was while staying at the White House that he developed his first serious crush on a girl. Maruja Mackehenie was a boarder at a Catholic school who stayed at the hotel during her holidays. His brother Bruce remembered, "his surrender was instant, absolute and agonizing. I could see that her mere appearance made him almost faint with longing."

However, Patrick's somewhat complicated, ambivalent attitude towards the opposite sex was revealed in letters to his brother at this time when he confessed to a predilection for "yearning" rather than for actual sexual fulfilment – "falling in love with the idea of love". He likened his feelings to those of Shelley, "I have an idea that he was oddly sexed – in rather the way that I am. Although clearly he slept with girls, I don't think this was what he was really after. I think he liked yearning for them – spooning. What he really enjoyed was the emotion I had for Maruja."

Maruja herself remembered Patrick as "extremely shy, unsure of himself, and unhappy", and nothing came of the liaison. However, her brother, Charles, soon became a close friend. He was handsome, urbane, cheerfully cynical, and an uncomplicated and untormented womaniser. In fact, he was something of a fantasy-figure for Patrick. On their forays into the West End, Charles (who would eventually become Peru's ambassador to the United Nations) introduced Patrick to social drinking and the seamier side of life in general. Patrick's drinking, soon to become a dominant feature in his life and work, started in earnest around this time.

In the autumn of 1922, aged 17, he was given a recommendation by Sutton Vane, his brother-in-law, to work as an actor and assistant stage manager for Andrew Melville II, one of a theatrical family whose connections with the stage went back to 1760. In 1922 Melville became actor-manager of the Grand Theatre, Brighton presenting, writing and acting in melodramas such as *The Reign of Terror*, *Dracula*, *Jack the Ripper* and *Sweeney Todd*. These pulled in the audiences and for many years The Grand was the town's most popular theatre. As a member of Melville's repertory company both in Brighton and the provinces, Hamilton was able to study the technique of melodrama closely. He realised how successful and effective his own plays might be if written and presented in, as he put it to his brother, "a sophisticated way" with a strong, simple, central idea, a single set and a small cast.

In September 1923, yet again Sutton Vane played a significant part in his brother-in-law's life. Vane's play, *Outward Bound*, proved to be an unexpected hit. From Hampstead in London it transferred to the West End before reaching New York's Broadway with an all-star cast that included Leslie Howard. It earned Vane a considerable amount of money and transformed both his and his immediate family's lifestyle.

Subsidised and encouraged by his brother-in-law, Patrick promptly gave up his itinerant jobbing existence and moved into lodgings in West Kensington where he began writing his first novel in earnest. As he explained to his brother, writing, unlike ordinary work which involved being stimulated by the presence and activities of others, was like "hard labour in 'solitary' – something to which even illness is preferable". His routine working life as a writer when actually engaged on a novel or play, would now and for the next 25 years, remain more or less the same. He would retreat into a cloistered place, rising each day at six-thirty in the morning to work, retiring to bed by nine-thirty in the evening. During such times he would not smoke and, if he went out in the evenings, he would limit himself to no more than three drinks.

The result of this first sustained literary assault was a novel called *Monday Morning*. Although it was largely autobiographical, it did possess significant technical strengths that would thereafter characterise his work. Apart from demonstrating the author's acute ear for dialogue, skilfully written set pieces occur containing fine delineation of character and a keen sense of pace.

It was eventually accepted by the publisher Constable in March 1925, and received some warm reviews. *The Sunday Times*' critic wrote: "A wholly delightful and charmingly impudent piece of work. Its first chapter puts the reader into the best of good tempers and its last finds him in the same agreeable mood."

This first success brought him new friends and broadened his social life. One of Constable's directors, Michael Sadleir, although 16 years older and an Oxford graduate, soon became one of Hamilton's closest friends. He would introduce him to a wider literary world, afford him entry to various exclusive clubs and, along with his assistant at Constable, Martha Smith, would form part of a dedicated drinking circle that would endure for many years.

Almost immediately, Hamilton turned to writing his next novel – this time drawing upon his experiences in the various boarding houses where he and his family had occasionally been forced into living during the past few years. *Craven House* was the result and, when he submitted it in 1926, his publishers were so pleased with it that they offered him a five-book contract and a guaranteed income of £100 a year. They knew what they were doing: the book was an instant bestseller, and made Hamilton's name both in Britain and America.

At this point his brother, Bruce, left for Barbados where he had found a teaching job in a college. The brothers would keep in touch over the succeeding years via letters and occasional visits, but the division between them was now set. Though Bruce would produce a number of commercially successful novels he would also have to teach to make ends meet. Patrick, by contrast, could now afford to lead the life of a professional novelist.

Within a year, his third novel, *Tuppence Coloured*, appeared. Set in the backstage of a theatre and based on Patrick's own brief acting career (and his sister's more extensive one), it featured an innocent heroine who is determined to become an actress. A narrowly-focused piece of writing, its satire was directed entirely at the trivia of life on

7

the stage and was so accurate and biting that it upset some in the theatrical profession. However, although highly thought of by his publisher, the reviews were no more than mildly encouraging.

But Hamilton was now established and successful enough not to worry unduly about *Tuppence*'s relative failure. Within a couple of years, he would produce the first of his enduring masterpieces, *Twenty Thousand Streets Under the Sky*, and enter the pantheon of great London novelists.

Craven House

Hamilton's world is one in which everyone is either a torturer or a victim – and in some cases both.

Nigel Jones, biographer

Craven House, the second of Hamilton's novels, established him as a writer of promise. He would always remain fond of it and many years later, when revising it for reissue, felt he could hardly change a line of it.

The time period covered in the book spans the decades either side of the First World War. It starts slowly with a series of portraits of the 'guests' staying at Craven House, Miss Hatt's boarding-house establishment in Chiswick, West London. It's probably difficult for a modern audience to fully comprehend the claustrophobic living arrangements tolerated by Miss Hatt's lodgers. These were a collection of failing members of the lower-middle class, ex-First World War officers and old Edwardians who had survived into the alien, servantless world of the 1920s and 1930s existing on their savings and annuities.

Apart from Miss Hatt, there is her old school friend, Mrs Spicer, and her husband (who might have married Miss Hatt). Next are the widowed Mrs Nixon and her daughter Elsie; then there's the widower, Major Wildman and his son Henry. Minor characters include domestic servant, Audrey, and cook Edith – not to mention Mac the parrot: "whose prevailing mood was one of good-tempered caustic bitterness against its captors – a mood which its abundance of years had served to emphasise rather than soften. It bit you when it could."

Their personal foibles and eccentricities, tawdry secrets, petty quarrels and reconciliations form the bulk of the text. As time passes, their hidden natures come to light. The outwardly respectable Mr Spicer is shown engaging in pub-crawls and seeking out prostitutes, Elsie's mother is revealed as a vicious tyrant wielding a stick upon her petrified daughter, while Miss Hatt's repressed contempt for her guests will eventually explode into comic violence.

Eventually one begins to grasp the excruciating embarrassment of having to spend one's life – eating, relaxing, growing up – in the intimate company of those with whom one has no real relationship and to whom one has very little of interest to say. In that sense, the 'social geography' may be strange but the psychology remains universal and Hamilton reveals himself as an expert in carefully delineating the sheer awfulness of such a situation, as well as exploiting opportunities to create painfully humiliating moments. Hell, in Hamilton's fiction, really is other people.

The "Long Evening Problem" is an early example. The original trio, Miss Hatt and the Spicers, find themselves, after the first few months of the arrangement, living in close proximity to one another and having to kill time following each evening meal. Having 'exhausted' the piano (Mrs Spicer plays classical excerpts), having made the weekly trip to the cinema and having sat watching the fire in silence just once too often, "the evenings were reaching a pitch of ennui and amiability almost intolerable – if not positively approaching the danger mark." Finally, the Spicers choose to simply ignore Miss Hatt, he reading the paper, she a novel. Miss Hatt's desperate forays into chitchat eventually founder and she is obliged to retreat to her room and bed. As Hamilton puts it, it was "the first cross word between them", and Miss Hatt's long, slow burn towards an incandescent finale is just one of a number of sub-plots he begins to weave into the mix.

But *Craven House* isn't simply about its petty bourgeois inhabitants. Also depicted, although in rather unreal and somewhat 'cocknified' style, is the world of the 'below stairs' domestic servant. The episode in which Audrey is summarily dismissed after many years of service for no more than a cheeky riposte to Miss Hatt, suggests where Hamilton's ultimate sympathies will lie.

Eventually, however, we find we are following the fortunes of the small boy, Master Henry Wildman, whom we see growing up.

Hamilton's experiences at Holland House School are now put to good use: Henry arrives at the new school, is mercilessly bullied in his first few days, accused of being a sneak, of cheating and cribbing, of stealing, is put 'on trial', reduced to tears, and tormented. By the following week, however, just like Hamilton, he is perfectly happy – having not conquered the bullies but become one of them.

Henry's father eventually dies, Henry leaves school and gets a job, and ultimately falls in love with an attractive but unsuitable girl, Miss Cotterell – the first of Hamilton's femme fatale creations. It's only in the last few pages of the novel that Henry realises that he loves, not Miss Cotterell but Elsie Nixon, with whom he has grown up and shared certain key moments. Elsie's forlorn love for Henry provides one of the book's main sub-texts. His own equally forlorn pursuit of another is a pattern that would re-emerge in *Twenty Thousand Streets Under the Sky* and *Slaves of Solitude*.

The relationship between Elsie and her awful mother underscores the evolving love-story. Elsie is repressed and afraid of her mother, and it is Henry's (apparently disinterested) insistence that she assert herself, that provides the book's dénouement. She takes a surreptitious trip to the West End shops, has her hair bobbed, buys herself an expensive dress with which to go to a party, thus overcoming her tyrannical mother who has forbidden her all these things.

The scene in which she finally confronts her mother is powerful, cathartic and perfectly realised: Elsie breaks the stick in half with which her mother has beaten her, exacting revenge on the child-tormentor through the 'confiscation' of her weapon; she finds exactly the right words at last to exorcise her maddening memories; all the while remaining perfectly composed as she warns her mother never to treat her again in such a way:

> "Give me that stick!"
> "All right. I'll give it to you," says Elsie, and seizes it firmly in both her Amazon hands. It breaks with a sound snap.
> "There you are," says Elsie.
> Mrs Nixon is now making choking noises on the bed.
> "It's no use your getting hysterical," says Elsie … "It's no use your getting hysterical …"
> There is an interval in which Mrs Nixon becomes more hysterical still, but nevertheless succeeds in muttering certain

not very clear imprecations under her breath.

"I'm tall now," says Elsie, in misty tones, and really looks it, as she stands there, for the first time in her life. "Taller than you. And I'm young. I'm young. And you're not going to make me old any more. I'm sorry if I was rude, but I'm not going to be made old any more!"

However, the ultimate explosion occurs during what turns out to be the final dinner at *Craven House*. It involves everyone, including an ugly, clearly 'fascistic' character – Mrs Nixon's unpleasant Scottish son whom she eventually brings along to enforce Elsie's obedience. He boasts of beating up a working class 'agitator', the first of a number of such 'politically' charged individuals who appear in Hamilton's fiction.

It is the proprietress, Miss Hatt's, scene, however, when she finally explodes. She throws food, denounces Mr Spicer and ends by finally dismissing them all. Craven House is to be closed. She can stand them all no more. They depart and it is at this point that Elsie and Henry finally discover they love one another. Their heart-warming coming together at the very end in the deserted Craven House is unusual in Hamilton's fiction and considered a weakness by some of his critics. It is an example of what Hamilton himself called "a country dance" – a simple life-affirming scene designed to round off a book and leave his readers well satisfied which, arguably, it does very well. Hamilton wrote many years later, "In a book of this sort, a little sentimentality is probably all to the good."

On a more intriguing note, what *Craven House* demonstrates on a stylistic level is Hamilton's predilection for almost total authorial control, the novel being a perfect example of what the Russian linguist and literary critic, Mikhail Bakhtin, terms a "monological text". This depends on the centrality of a single authoritative voice, where all confirmed ideas are merged in the unity of the author's seeing and representing consciousness. The one who knows, understands and sees is in the first instance the author himself. Witness the scene when Elsie is saying her prayers [my italics]:

> Thus cleansed and prepared, she kneels down by the bed, closes her eyes and purses her mouth *like a little girl about to receive a blow*, clasps her hands, and prays. Her prayer *has*

little esoteric significance for her. She prays that a certain *hazy* Kingdom may come (*inwardly trusting that nothing will supersede the United Kingdom in her own lifetime*); she prays for this day's bread (*discrepantly, for it is already granted*) and to have her trespasses forgiven. (Elsie can never quite place her own Trespasses, but *has a vague belief* that one is Prosecuted if they aren't forgiven.) And all this to a candlelit room with *softly jocund and perfectly cynical shadows*. She then jumps into her chilly bed, *a little white bundle of self-chastened original sin*, snuffs out the candle, and vaguely hopes for salvation in the dark.

Hamilton deploys what is termed Free Indirect Discourse, where words represent a consciousness, a subjectivity, a particular perspective on the world around them and on themselves, which allows his narrative voice to slip in and out of various perspectives on the action. Terms such as "It appears ..." or "it seems that" posit questions: it appears or seems to whom? Whose vocabulary is this? Whose perspective is this? Invariably, it is the author's, although sharing his thoughts and confidences with the reader at the expense of the character.

Here is Mr Spicer appearing late for dinner, in a drunken state:

> That Mr Spicer is still in a fuddled condition there is no doubt. *Whether, however, Mr Spicer allows the company to detect this condition in him, is another matter.* And apart from the fact that Mrs Spicer seems to be indulging in more "Yesses", and "No's", and "Certainlies", out-of-hand to the Universe than she has ever been known to do before, *it would appear* that Mr Spicer preserves his secret intact.
> *We* are nevertheless bound to remark that Mr Spicer's treatment of the joint is a little hazy and perplexed: that, having worked in a maladroit manner upon a problematical slice of lamb, he at last succeeds in furnishing his plate with oddments, and then sits down at short notice: that, having sat down, he immediately rises, grasps the utensils, says "More for anybody? No? No more for anybody?" and takes his time about sitting down this time: and that although conversation is maintained during the rest of supper, and Mr Spicer gives his share to it, in the silences that do happen to fall, Mr Spicer *is to be sensed distantly, and perhaps inaudibly, hiccoughing.*

It is a technique that sometimes can seem suffocating, his characters at times appearing to be mere marionettes whose strings he pulls – and we, the readers, can see those strings!

Nevertheless, *Craven House* contains within its narrow confines almost all the topics and themes that would occupy Hamilton for the rest of his writing career: the public house and the effects of drink; forlorn love for a femme fatale; prostitutes; and above all, petty bourgeoisie suburban fascism.

2

Rush to Fame: London Laid Bare

1928-1934 Literary and stage triumph, worldwide fame, and tragedy.
Twenty Thousand Streets Under The Sky, The Midnight Bell, The Siege of Pleasure, The Plains of Cement

The period that followed Hamilton's first major writing success finally marked the end of his sporadic periods of living at home, where times had certainly changed. With no money now to pay for servants, his mother was becoming increasingly disgruntled and difficult. Hamilton began to spend a great deal of his non-writing time drinking with friends and frequenting the Soho area of London with a view to seeking out prostitutes.

Physical sex would always be a problem for him. He admitted to his brother that he'd avoided involvement with women when he was a young actor in spite of there being plenty of opportunities. As we have seen, he could experience powerful feelings, such as those for Maruja, but he struggled to satisfy them. In the summer of 1927 these problems would have a powerful impact on both his life and his writing career when he met a prostitute called Mrs Lily Connolly. He plunged into an affair with her that tormented and degraded him, leaving him physically and emotionally exhausted. He later admitted in letters to his brother that it had been a terrible experience during which he had become involved in "brawls at restaurants and fights in the street" and had "fallen among thieves in Soho dens".

In 1928, his father once again moved back into the family home, ill, and needing to be cared for. In order to distance himself, Patrick now moved out for good, to 50a New Cavendish Street, which was closer to the West End haunts he continued to frequent. Here, he commenced the novel *The Midnight Bell* which he finished in June 1928.

Fashioned out of his previous experiences with Mrs Connolly, it is a powerful work, a painfully honest study of infatuation and humiliation. A young barman called Bob falls for an even younger prostitute called Jenny who, over the course of just a few days, manages to spend every penny that Bob has carefully saved over the years. It was the first in a trilogy of novels that would eventually be published under the title, *Twenty Thousand Streets Under The Sky*, one of Hamilton's greatest achievements.

The Midnight Bell would prove to be an instant success. The *Times Literary Supplement* reviewer was enthusiastic: "Mr Hamilton holds his reader by his accomplished writing, his gift for realistic portraiture, his pitiless refusal to cast any befogging glamour over what can only be falsely romanticised and, not least, by his ability to make the least of his characters real personalities and to make their personalities the motive forces of his story."

However, between its completion and appearance in the bookshops, Hamilton was to score a major triumph in another important artistic arena. Like his brother-in-law before him, he had written a play – *Rope* – which was destined to become an instant success in the West End of London and beyond.

It wasn't his first foray into producing something for the stage. In 1927 he had written an unpublished piece entitled, 'The World for Which Men Work' about a poor, unmarried couple who are transported to a Utopia. *Rope* appeared in 1929 from almost nowhere as he told his bemused brother (still in Barbados). He'd written it on scraps of paper in pubs and in Lyons Corner Houses. His personal theatrical connections had helped by getting it swiftly passed to a producer. After a successful try-out it was soon transferred to the West End where it ran for many months.

The genesis of the play (a point later denied by Hamilton) was said to be an actual American murder trial which took place in 1924 involving two young friends with a naïve enthusiasm for Nietzsche. They had kidnapped a younger friend and murdered him before trying to extract a ransom from his parents. Hamilton developed this theme, adding a macabre twist – after murdering their friend, the two young men place his body in a chest and invite friends and the boy's relatives round for tea. This was served on the chest!

Despite suggestions that the play represented a working-through of Hamilton's own deep interest in the philosophy of Nietzsche, he insisted that *Rope* was nothing more than pure entertainment. He commented, "It's a thriller, a thriller of all time, and nothing but a thriller." In the foreword to the published play he wrote, "I have gone all out to write a horror play and make your flesh creep. And there is no reason to believe that this reaction is medically or chemically any worse for you than making you laugh or cry. If I have succeeded, you will leave the theatre braced and recreated, which is what you go to the theatre for."

Nevertheless, some critics were to find the play's theme obscene and objectionable; others, more prosaically, rejoiced in its lack of the usual props. *The Nation* critic wrote "A murder play without pistols, knives and spooks is a very distinguished relief; also the author was really talking about something the whole time." *Rope* was to have another life as a classic film some years later.

On a purely practical level, the play made Hamilton a lot of money – between £30 and £40 a week. This, and the critically acclaimed reception of *The Midnight Bell*, made him a famous writer. His social life was increasingly taken up with seeing agents, producers and publishers – as well as his usual hard drinking and general carousing.

By stark contrast, the affairs of his family members seemed to be declining rapidly. His brother returned from Barbados and succeeded in getting his first novel published but the two had drifted apart, certainly in terms of the worlds each inhabited. His sister's marriage was now in trouble as her husband's successes dried up. A divorce would soon follow and she began a long, painful decline into alcoholism. To round things off, their father died – un-mourned by any of them.

Then in 1930, much to everyone's surprise, Hamilton announced that he was married. He had met Lois Martin – a strikingly handsome, cultured and accomplished woman – at a party given by J.B. Priestley. She was three years older than Patrick and the union at first promised to solve many of his social and sexual problems. It proved in time, however, to be a mixed blessing.

The couple moved into a new flat in Upper Berkeley Street, London, W1, but soon, predictably, differences between them began to manifest themselves. They discovered that they were sexually incompatible, which was exacerbated by Hamilton's inevitable recourse to ever heavier drinking. Eventually, various compromises were arrived at and the couple managed to co-habit in a long, companionable, but platonic relationship. Hamilton did, however, stipulate that his life beyond the marriage would continue as if he were *not* married, claiming complete personal liberty for himself.

His work schedule had continued apace, and he produced a new play, *John Brown's Body*, which wasn't a success and made only a short appearance on stage. By July 1931, however, he had finished the second novel in the *Twenty Thousand Streets* series, *The Siege of Pleasure*. This looks back to how Jenny, Bob's *l'amour fou*, became a prostitute in the first place. Initially working as a household servant, she spends an evening drinking in a pub with some shady characters who promise her a career as a model. Unable to resist, she acquiesces and eventually drifts into prostitution.

While waiting for the book to appear, Hamilton adapted *Rope* for radio. This was his first move into a medium then in its infancy and for which he would produce some interesting, if perhaps unchallenging, work over the years. Val Gielgud, then Head of Drama at the BBC, 'hyped' the forthcoming transmission of *Rope* and caused a minor storm. He issued a statement in the form of a three-minute warning talk, suggesting that the play might prove "too strong" for some listeners. A discussion followed in the newspapers about the advisability of transmitting it and the British Empire Union lodged a complaint which all made for very good publicity! When it was finally transmitted on the 18th January 1932 it was generally well-received.

But there now occurred a sudden and dramatic event that would affect the course of Hamilton's life in many ways. He had gone to stay with his sister in her flat in Earls Court, London over Christmas and, on the morning of Sunday, 24th January, as he walked out into Earls Court Road, a car careered across the road and carried him on its bonnet for several yards. His left arm was fractured above the elbow, his right thigh and wrist suffered compound fractures and there were multiple lacerations to his face and head. His forehead was deeply gashed and his nose almost torn off.

Though never in danger of death, he was left with a withered arm and a stiff leg that hampered his mobility and a permanently scarred face and a nose that, despite plastic surgery, was left an unsightly blob.

It is part of the Hamilton mythology that the accident affected him so much that it hastened his decline into alcoholism. He was permanently scarred, it is true, and the work on his nose was clumsy. As someone already quite sensitive about his appearance, this clearly did not help his self-esteem, but he was already a very heavy drinker and in later years, when discussing his alcoholism, the accident and its aftermath was never referred to. There were, in fact, some advantages to the accident. He sued for damages and was delighted to be awarded £6,000. When sufficiently recovered, he used the experience when he added a road accident scene to *The Siege of Pleasure* before it was published in late 1932.

At the beginning of 1933, he moved with his wife to stay at the Wells Hotel in Hampstead and began work on an adaptation of *The Midnight Bell* for the stage, though this would come to nothing. In January 1934, his mother, after a long illness and facing the prospect of blindness, killed herself with an overdose, an act expected and possibly even condoned by her children.

Hamilton left no record of the impact this distressing event had on his life, though it must have been considerable. For good or ill, she had been a force in his life, and she would surface every now and then in the various forms of his female characters. Is it a coincidence that one of his most impressive and sympathetic female characters, Ella, in the book he was currently engaged upon, almost shares his mother's maiden name?

He worked on regardless, however, following his customary, strict routine: "the same every day. Work, walk, lunch, sleep, Work, beer, supper, read" and finished *The Plains of Cement*, the third and final book of the *Twenty Thousand Streets* trilogy. This tells the story of the barmaid, Ella, who works with Bob in *The Midnight Bell* and is secretly in love with him. One of the pub's customers, Mr Eccles, is determined to marry her despite a significant difference in years between them. Ella's agonising choice provides the novel with its pathos and tension, but the fact that the action runs simultaneously with Bob's tortured affair with Jenny, provides the reader with an intriguing reworking of events. The conclusion of *The Plains of*

Cement, while certainly not a "country dance", furnishes these bleak portrayals of lonely London lives with a moving, even inspiring, climax.

The trilogy was published in 1935 under the collective title *Twenty Thousand Streets Under the Sky* and marked the end of a significant phase in Hamilton's life and work. It would be another seven years before he would produce another novel of similar quality. He would not, however, be idle during those years.

Twenty Thousand Streets Under the Sky

> *It is the poet's business to put into words the universal wail of humanity at not being able to get everything it wants exactly when it wants it.*
>
> Patrick Hamilton

In 1927, Hamilton wrote to his brother:

> Lately I've been making the most extraordinary expeditions into Soho – mixing a great deal with the courtesans therein, and also the low life. I think I've got an idea for an extraordinary and really valuable novel. I daresay you know it's always been one of my leading ambitions to write about the life of servants – particularly female ones – and their oppressed hideous condition. And it's also been my ambition to write about harlots. I have two first-rate novels with either of these subjects. Now my latest adventures have led me into remarkable social observations and enlightenments, and it's suddenly occurred to me that to write a novel which is both about servants and harlots (possibly the slow transformation of one into the other) would not only be ferociously good as a novel, but really sound work.

The three novels making up the *Twenty Thousand Streets* trilogy demonstrate the distance between an author's declared aim and the actual realisation of that aim. The "sound work" Hamilton refers to suggests that the novels were to serve a practical purpose rather than merely entertain. Having become an enthusiastic Marxist during the writing of the trilogy, his belief that society was in the last throes of capitalist decline had certainly begun to affect the way he approached his work. How far the novels serve any overt political purpose, however, is arguable. There is no political activity in the trilogy and if the reader is expecting to find an exposé of the "oppressed hideous conditions" of the working class he/she will be disappointed.

The books do, in fact, make an invaluable contribution to the fiction of London life and its inhabitants – what he called "the weird teeming aquarium of the metropolis". More importantly, however, they allow him to expound and develop his own deeply felt ideas on the dilemma of being alive. He explained to his brother: "this is a bloody awful life, that we are none of us responsible for our own lives and actions, but merely in the hands of the gods, that nature don't care a damn ... and whether you're making love, being hanged, or getting drunk, it's all a futile way of passing the time in the brief period allotted to us preceding death."

The Midnight Bell

Centred around a pub on the Euston Road, *The Midnight Bell* focuses upon the inner life of the barman, Bob, as he falls in love with Jenny, a West End prostitute. We follow his descent into self-inflicted despair as he is continually let down by this shallow, scheming woman and loses all sense of any reality (not to mention all his savings) in the face of his obsession. Hamilton had, at this point, himself become embroiled in the demeaning affair with the prostitute, Lily Connolly ("my latest adventures"), and the experiences continued to provide him with plenty of raw material.

Bob is presented as a good-natured and affable 25-year-old ex-merchant seaman. He's an orphan, his mother having died when he was a teenager at sea, his father someone he never knew. As the bar door opens on the morning in question, a pretty girl walks in – modelled, Hamilton later confessed – on one of the Hamilton brothers' favourite film stars.

It is immediately clear from the reactions of everyone in the bar that she is a street-walker, but Bob is entranced. Her transparently bogus sob-story (she claims she is ill, but owes rent and must 'work' that night regardless) gives Bob his chance. Hamilton notes, however, that his attempt to keep her off the streets for a night makes him feel, "dreadfully conceited. He was so innocent as to believe the transaction was almost unique ... He was in love with himself". By closing time, he has given her 10 shillings to pay her rent, and has begun his rapid descent into the hell that his creator had so recently had been toiling in.

Unusually for someone so young and itinerant, Bob possesses a considerable amount of money, carefully saved and stored in the Midland Bank in Tottenham Court Road. This cache, we are told, gives him "more pleasure than anything else in the world".

From the first moment we are told about it, it is clear that by the time this incongruous encounter is over, the money will be gone. Thus, we watch with fascinated horror as he slowly but surely hands it over, Jenny all the while making tortuous but obviously empty protests. Despite her apparent shallowness, she is nevertheless endowed with a cold, calculating sense of just how far and fast she can go in order to get as much as she can from her puppy-like admirer and little by little Bob's precious security falls into her lap, wasted on drink and 'loans' and even on a new blue suit that he vainly hopes will impress her.

It's an odd courtship, however, as Bob, though clearly no virgin (according to the text we are told he had been to sea, and "his behaviour had been neither eccentric nor snobbish in foreign ports") appears to have no carnal interest in Jenny at all. The idea that he might avail himself of what she actually sells never seems to cross his mind. It's been suggested by Professor McKenna that he is perhaps more erotically fascinated by the contradictions generated by her social identity as a prostitute, that is, she's so attractive because she's been possessed by so many others. That she is also married only adds to this allure. As evidence that his motives aren't quite as altruistic as they appear on the surface, McKenna points to the fact that Bob fantasises about returning to sea in order to "cleanse" himself.

Throughout the telling of the tale, the reader is in what one critic has called "the terrible grip" of Hamilton's prose and the trilogy marks a significant step forward in his literary style. His use of short sentences and chapters, the employment of dots and dashes, drive the narrative forward with an urgency matching the desperation of Bob's plight as he plunges ever more recklessly into the quagmire of his obsession.

Hamilton wrote to his brother, "I have developed a lot of new theories about writing and style, the latter having acquired a peculiar penchant for short sentences – not staccato – but a little shorter and crisper even than can be observed in the last chapter of the first book of *Tuppence Coloured* – the best thing I ever wrote, I still maintain, at least in the serious line."

His use of narrated monologue or free indirect discourse in the representation of fictional consciousness, is a mixture of psycho-narration and interior monologue. Thus the narrator often sets the scene but the character's thoughts are reproduced 'directly' and in a way that one would imagine the character to think. Although the narrator continues to talk of the character in the third person, the syntax becomes less formal by the use of incomplete sentences, exclamations, etc. Thus, the character's mind style is reproduced more closely.

Hamilton said, "There are no comic 'Kapital Letters' in the new book, I work a great deal with the dash and colon, and am not afraid of awkward rhythms."

Here, for instance, Bob has managed to trace Jenny down after their first meeting and he buys her a drink:

> There was another silence. She sipped her drink, he watched her. She was awfully pretty. Whatever her sins, he and she were both young. He saw a man, at a near table, looking at her. She really didn't look like one – in here and in the company of a man. Last night he was her deliverer. He felt unaccountably proud and satisfied.
> "Couldn't we go round there?" he said.
> "What – 'The Globe'?"
> "Yes."
> "Well, we could, they don't start dancin' till eleven, though."
> "Well, we'll go there when the time comes. What about it?"
> "Fine," she said.
> She was a bit of a puzzle. She had a way of suddenly taking things rather for granted. His mind fled darkly and rapidly into a contemplation of his own resources. He should get out of the 'Globe' on ten shillings, and five shillings should cover the drinks, etc., before that fifteen shillings. Apart from a little loose change, he had two pounds on him, both of which were

to have been deposited at the Midland Bank on Monday. But, he reflected, you only lived once, and not long at that.

The 'voices' of both the narrator and the character are momentarily merged. This can create an impression of immediacy but it can also be used to introduce an element of irony, when the reader realises that a character is misguided without actually being told so by the narrator.

As critic and biographer Laura Thompson has pointed out, in *The Midnight Bell*, we are afforded an overview of Bob's folly, being taken through every step of the folly *as seen by the characters themselves*. When Bob scatters his proudly earned eighty pounds upon "the barren soil of Jenny's favour", we can see exactly how he is thinking, the logic with which he is pursuing his illogical end, and the apparent control he has over his *lack of control*. As Thompson says, "We are with him every doomed step along the road that he believes himself to be travelling *of his own free will*. Hamilton never misses a single stage of the process of obsession; he doggedly fills in what most writers would omit, and thus he achieves his extraordinary grip upon the reader." Hamilton writes that, one morning, "Bob came to a new theory of Money" and would "henceforward regard himself as a man with seventy-five pounds behind him instead of eighty". Reading this, we instantly fear the worst.

Aside from the principal narrative, *The Midnight Bell* provides us with a portrait of a London pub, its staff and its patrons in the 1920s that is wonderfully rich. It captures the oddness of life on both sides of the bar, a perfect example of the fruits of Hamilton's labours in pubs and taverns the length and breadth of the capital when he would sit quietly in a corner listening and observing for hours.

The writer Claud Cockburn wrote of this same characteristic: "Often standing with Hamilton in a London bar our conversation would suddenly be interrupted by Patrick suffering what seemed a minor convulsion or rictus. Seeing my astonishment he would say, "But, my God, didn't you hear what that man said; don't you see the sort of thing he is up to? God help us." The man in question, with his back to us, was probably seven or eight feet away but Patrick had not only heard what he said but actually interpreted it. Two or three times I rather meanly tested him on this by waiting until he had left the pub and scraping acquaintance with the stranger. On each occasion the man's opinions proved to be precisely what Hamilton had deduced with his bat's wing ear."

Simon Goulding, in his article 'Fitzrovian Nights', delineates the specific nature of space in Hamilton's public houses, that of the saloon bar in particular and the behaviour and significance of the characters Hamilton has chosen to place there.

Among the Bell's regulars are Mr Sounder, who writes letters to the papers bemoaning the short cropped hairstyles of "the would-be modern young miss", even though he has "rather more hair coming in two exact little sprouts from his nostrils than modern fashion allows or nicety dictates." There's Mr Wall, with his excruciating rhymes and wordplay; and there's the mysterious Mr McDonald, also known as Illegal Operation who was

> ... about thirty-two, and wore grey flannel trousers, a sports coat, rather dirty shirts, and knitted ties. He had sandy hair, rather closely cropped (as though he had acquired the habit in prison and rather fancied the style) and grey eyes. He had enormous ears, and a long nose with a rather bashed in appearance – an illegal nose in fact, and a full mouth and a large chin. Every now and again he tried to commit suicide, but could never manage to bring it off. Despite all these things, he really wouldn't hurt a fly and was quite a good fellow if you didn't rub him up the wrong way.

McDonald, like so many of the pub's habitués, inhabits his own small space and makes little attempt at genuine social intercourse. When in a conversation he is described as, "listening to the other (which took place very seldom)" his replies, being merely drunken slurs, such as "Jussfussy". He's as isolated as Mr Wall, a man, "obscurely connected with motors in Great Portland Street" ... "a very sprightly little man ... [h]e had a red face, fair hair, twinkling blue eyes, a comic little moustache and a bowler hat".

Goulding has suggested that two details stand out: the red face, symbolic of excessive alcohol consumption, and the bowler hat – one of the classic symbols of the English middle class, and one which

Hamilton would later employ to greater effect in his comic novel *Impromptu in Moribundia*. Wall indulges endlessly in what he calls "tomfooleries":

> It was a patter in the conditional. Similarly, in his own particular idiom, Martyrs were associated with Tomatoes, Waiters with Hot Potatoes, Cribbage with Cabbage, Salary with Celery (the entire vegetable world was ineffably droll), Suits with Suet, Fiascos with Fiancées and the popular wireless genius with Macaroni. He was perhaps, practically off his head.

Though we may feel momentarily sorry for Wall as he desperately (but irritatingly) twists everyone's words when not actually being spoken to, his dogged insistence also suggests something of the bully about him. What's more, his prolonged periods at the bar clearly indicate that he sees it as the only place where he has any real substance. Outside, he is another of the ghostly men walking the streets attempting to find some meaning in their lives, like the third of the trio, Mr Sounder, whose appearance was

> ... eccentric. Though of short stature he wore a thick beard and moustache which (though they did not in fact decrease his height) created an illusion of dwarfishness. This impression was augmented by the hair on his head, which went back in a thick mane, magnificent for his age, which was something over fifty ... He wore, and had worn for years without interruption, a thick tweed suit, a soft collar, and a heavy bow tie.

Sounder's description is the fullest of any of the bar regulars, suggesting to Goulding that he might well be composite of various Hamiltonian family traits; cadging drinks like Hamilton himself, living in Osnaburgh Terrace, as did his brother Bruce, or writing bad poetry similar to that of Hamilton's father, Bernard:

> Beginning with an impassioned apostrophe to the "fretted lights and tall aspiring *nave*", Mr Sounder went straight ahead to describe the music, which was coming in "wave on *wave*", and which in so doing (as we might have known) his "Soul did *lave*".

25

Bob's delusions and humiliations were Hamilton's, of course. Like Bob, Hamilton idolised and indulged his real-life prostitute/madonna and was also tossed nothing but empty promises in return for his devotion and sacrifice. Jenny repaid none of Bob's money, broke dates with impunity and simply discarded any promises that she would look for real work. Yet Bob forgave and forgot at the first false sign of affection on Jenny's part. Hamilton had been through it all himself and understood completely Bob's foolishness. It enabled him to write about the whole crazy situation with detachment and wry humour.

That Hamilton had gone through a similar experience is always cited as being of crucial importance: that his life produced rich material for fiction. However, though he may have recycled episodes from his own life, he significantly remade them, imposing a fictional pattern on them for his own purposes. He must have known, as he pursued Lily across London, that he was entering a world that was not his. She couldn't escape her existence as a prostitute and was condemned to stay. He could always escape back to his middle-class milieu. In that sense he was the powerful one in the relationship. What's more, in the second story of the trilogy, he was able to wreak fictional vengeance on his real-life tormentor.

The Siege of Pleasure

The Siege of Pleasure is Jenny's story, and we watch as she journeys from servant girl to prostitute in a few turbulent hours. It is little more than an extended short story, however, constructed along the lines of a cautionary tale. Her downfall is clinically observed by the monologic author who, while making her thoughts available to us, invites us to mock rather than sympathise with her.

Hamilton lays the responsibility squarely on the individual suggesting that it was doubtful whether Jenny could be said to be the owner of either a character or conscience:

> Her ignorance, her shallowness, her scheming self-absorption, her vanity, her callousness, her unscrupulousness – all these qualities – in combination with her extreme prettiness and her utter lack of harmony with her environment – were merely waiting and accumulating in heavy suspense in the realms of

respectability to be plunged down into the realms where they rightly belonged: and a single storm, lasting no longer than six hours achieved this.

Before our eyes, she changes from the demure, respectable servant who "knows her place" to a bold, careless, selfish slut who casually casts off her consumptive admirer, Tom, and throws in her lot with her new, car-driving, fast set.

The novel begins and ends with three elderly people living in a large house in Chiswick employing Jenny as a servant to replace an unsuitable one they have just dismissed. Jenny appears to be perfect, a "treasure" (echoing the dreams of Miss Hatt in *Craven House*) but within a day she is gone – and we follow what happens to her.

She is drawn into a drinking bout with a fun-loving friend, Violet, and three casual male pickups. The catalyst is, inevitably, drink, and Hamilton delineates with the skill of a life-long drinker her first experience of the transforming nature of alcohol: "She felt the port trickling down inside, and it seemed that a kind of light fell upon her."

In the course of a single night she gets drunk for the first time, rides in a car for the first time (which kills or injures a cyclist), spends her first night in the flat of a strange upper-class man and, although ashamed the next morning, decides not to go back to the old folk and "skivvying". The old folk are thus left to face their mortality. And Jenny her descent into the abyss:

> Silly old things – they had thought they were doing her a favour by engaging her. Favour indeed! – she'd show 'em. She was as good as them any day. She betted Andy had got as much money as them any day, and what mattered in these days save money? What were class distinctions nowadays? Relics of the past. She'd show 'em. She'd show everybody.

Hamilton had, however, written to his brother: "The cardinal fact is that women cannot earn a decent living (as people vaguely think they may). Their position, in fact, if one takes the trouble to examine it, and think hard about it, is hideous. I'm going into wages and facts. They are utterly dependant on their sexual attractions for their salvation. There never was such a need for a huge feminist movement as there is now. I can't explain, but this is so, and I think I have good work ahead."

For someone apparently concerned with the plight of working-class women, *The Siege of Pleasure* is a tale bereft of compassion or even deep social insight into the feminine psyche. It certainly tells us little about the situation of working women at the time, if that was his intention. (His "good work".)

Whether in domestic service or working as a prostitute, Jenny is not portrayed as being 'oppressed' in any way. She is admired and appreciated by the three old ladies. She appears confident and fully in control as she chooses prostitution of her own free will. She is not even under the thumb of a manipulating pimp. Her only demon is, and will probably continue to be, alcohol.

Jenny is a real, self-willed, albeit tragic little character, shallow and self-serving. In the third book of the trilogy, Hamilton creates an altogether more sympathetic female portrait.

The Plains of Cement

The Plains Of Cement (1934) runs parallel in time to *The Midnight Bell*, and follows the travails of the pub's good, straightforward barmaid, Ella, as she is relentlessly pursued by Mr Ernest Eccles, one of the pub's customers, the possessor of a new hat, a crooked front tooth and private financial means. Though their 'courtship' is comical to the reader, it is a horror story for poor Ella, who has to endure Eccles' incomprehensible mutterings while being pressed up against railings or squeezed on park benches, all the while struggling to cope with her sublimated love for Bob. Whilst the marriage would free her from her life of toil and the class in which she is trapped, it would simultaneously bind her to a man she dislikes. She ultimately refuses him, and is left alone to her bleak fate.

Ella, along with Miss Roach of *The Slaves of Solitude*, is one of Hamilton's finest fictional female achievements, at once real as well as being an archetype: She is able to "[talk] quietly to a customer at one end of the bar, or [move] about busily dispensing those distillations to whose existence and efficacy the whole building owed its origin and peculiar design." Hamilton's description continues: "she had no knowledge of the oddity of her station behind that bar –

a virtuous, homely, and simple-minded young woman, set up for five hours on end to withstand and feed the accumulating strength of the behaviour of scores upon scores of strange men manifestly out, or going out of their minds."

One of his biographers rightly says that Hamilton saw his job as a writer not just to purify the language but to find the poetry in the language that people use. Ella is an unwitting mouthpiece for that poetry. Hamilton says of her:

> The banality of the expressions she employed in voicing her thoughts was no criterion of those thoughts, real shrewdness or aptness. Infinitely stale and hackneyed idioms she certainly used, but this was merely because, having access to the wisdom of the ages, she used the expressions sanctified by the ages.

On the other hand, Mr Eccles is a lower middle-class man, dressed in the "conservative collars, ties and garments of a respectable middle-aged clerk". He is physically unprepossessing, "his bright blue eyes, his decided walk, his quick smile, his erect stature, the nervous turns of his body and movements of his arms, all said the same thing". Eccles is mildly satirised by Hamilton as petty-bourgeois. with his precious disposable income and his belief in thrift and sensible 'speculation'. But he is also shy and vulnerable, certainly not an inherently nasty character. However, because he is clearly preparing Ella for a particular role in his life, and because his mask occasionally slips to reveal definite traits of mild sexual sadism, the reader is always securely positioned on Ella's side.

Eccles does have one outstanding physical feature:

> Mr Eccles had a Tooth in his head. This was a large one right in the centre of the upper front row, and gained eminence in his mouth less from its size than from its crooked tendencies, insomuch as it came pointedly forth and hung down over the next tooth.

Its appearance distracts Ella whilst she is in conversation with him so that she loses track of what he's saying, her mind preoccupied with what a dentist might do to improve it. However, Eccles has a narcissistic preoccupation, as illustrated by his obsession with his new hat:

29

You could see at a glance that for the time being the man lived in and through his hat. You could see that it cost him sharp torture even to put it on his head, where he could not see it, and it had to take its chance. You could see him searching incessantly for furtive little glimpses of his hat in mirrors, you could see him adjusting his tie as a sort of salute to his hat, as an attempt to live up to his hat. You could see him striving to do none of these things.

He suggests that Ella is, in fact, responsible for him buying the new hat:

> "How am I responsible?" she added. "Eh?"
> "Well – you told me to get another – didn't you?"
> "Me? I didn't."
> "Yes, you did. Surely you remember."
> "I *didn't*," said Ella.
> "Oh yes, you did," said Mr Eccles. "Don't you remember telling me I ought to get a new one?"
> "Oh well," said Ella, "Ought … that's not telling you."
> "Well I thought so. I took it as a command."
> Oh, why wouldn't Bob come in, thought Ella.
> "It's not for me," she said, "to command you."
> "Oh – isn't it?" said Mr Eccles in the vague and preoccupied tone of one whose intentions of dalliance with her were now too manifest to be disputed.
> "Are you interested," said Mr Eccles, "in the theatre at all?"

A great deal of fun is derived from these verbal 'battles'. Their relationship receives its fullest and most eloquent expression in the dialogue, unwinding in repetitions, clichés and misunderstandings, the exchanges "repeating and accumulating like minimalist music". Hamilton works relentlessly away at the repetitive idiocy of conversation until he finds its pathos and poetry:

> "Oh well," says Ella, desperately seeking a breathing space as Eccles grimly flirts with her.
> "Oh well what?" he counters. "What do you mean? Oh well, what?"
> "Oh, just 'Oh well, what.'"
> "I'm afraid I don't know what you mean."

"You said, 'Oh well', so I asked you what you were thinking of."
"Oh well, one often says 'Oh well' – doesn't one?"
"Does one?"

Eccles baffles and bewilders poor Ella who desperately seeks to make sense of the man and his intentions. At such times she can occasionally appear maddeningly blinkered, unable or unwilling to see what we can see – that he wishes to marry her. Instead, she torments herself by poring over every slight nuance, ever freighted word, wondering if she is behaving correctly towards him. Hamilton allows her a complex internal life, one that might seem at odds with her simple outward demeanour. That her thoughts often continue well beyond the timespan available to think them, nonetheless enhances the psychological depth, not to say uniqueness, of this his finest female creation.

Despite Hamilton's strictures against the Modernist movement, his trilogy is anything but traditional in the structural sense. The three volumes are concerned with the same story told from different people's points of view and incorporate extensive rendering of their inner lives using Free Indirect Style. The second story precedes the first, which it explains, and the third occurs roughly simultaneously with the first. Although the books can stand entirely independent of each another, we become aware through Ella's story that the trilogy sometimes treats actual *episodes* from different points of view. Also, as we read the third story, our pre-knowledge of episodic events emphasises the sense in which the characters are somehow trapped inside the goldfish bowls of their lives with little chance of affecting their futures. This complicated structural device, controlled with perfect balance by Hamilton, greatly enhances the true power he has over his deceptively complex social and psychological storylines.

A good example of this is the telling (in *The Midnight Bell*) and retelling (in *The Plains of Cement*) of Ella's rejection for a job as a nanny in India by E. Sanderson-Chantry, the wife of a colonial official. Ella is interviewed and appears to have the job, but has to wait a day or two for confirmation as another girl has first refusal. In *The Midnight Bell*, Bob is informed by Ella that she might be leaving to go to India. It is clear she is telling him in order to see how he reacts, to discover whether he'll be disappointed, maybe even make a move for her. He doesn't, however, and more or less tells her that she should take the chance. A day later:

> Bob began on the brass as usual and Ella came down a little later. Her nose was very pink and her first news was in accordance with the general atmosphere of the day. India was Off. She had had a letter only that morning. She took it well, but it had an effect on Bob as well as herself. A fog obliterated the Universe and India was Off. The imprisoning and inescapable factors of existence made themselves felt. India was off. Would anything ever be on again?

In *The Plains of Cement*, we get the full story and, of course, Ella's perspective when she receives the news that she's not been chosen:

> India was Off – that was the burden that lay on her soul all the long dark day. She wished she had not told Bob about it, as she now had to tell him that it was Off. He was sympathetic, but he had his own thoughts to attend to, and she could see he had no comprehension of the desolation of a fog-ridden world in which India was Off.

Giving the episode more prominence simply underlines how little insight the characters have of one another's feelings and motivations. Contrary to Bob's reading of her reaction, Ella does not "take it well". We see how hard it hits her in *The Plains of Cement*, but at that stage we, the readers, are at an advantage over her – we know long before Ella does that India will be "Off".

Eccles offers Ella an escape from the tedious drudgery of her present life. Hamilton reveals that she comes from Pimlico, at the time a shabby working-class district of London. She was born into poverty and can expect little else. What's more, from our reading of *The Midnight Bell*, we know how hopeless her dreams of marriage to Bob are. Eccles, as Ella constantly reminds him, is from a significantly higher social class, living as he does in Chiswick, and possessing a "military" background. As evidence of the yawning social gap between them, it is revealed that Ella's brother also had military connections: but as a private in the Great War, one of the thousands to have perished there.

As the courtship proceeds Ella finds opportunities to better herself come and go: her stepfather falls ill and is expected to die and leave her downtrodden mother and herself a considerable amount of money. But he recovers. The offer of a job as a nanny also comes and goes. All the while, she watches Bob from afar, disapproving of his involvement with prostitutes ("them creatures"). Finally, on Christmas day, she discovers he has left the pub for good and has not even said goodbye. Heartbroken, she writes a letter to Eccles rejecting him forever, and goes to the cinema alone. Unable to post the letter, she struggles along the wet streets – and by chance meets Bob. But, unlike the meeting of Master Wildman and Elsie at the end of *Craven House*, which results in reconciliation and happiness, there is no salvation for Ella, no "country dance". Bob is merely killing time before leaving on a merchant ship. The sorry pair have tea together, and make their stumbling farewells. Before parting, Ella gives Bob the letter to post. Though desperately sad and moving, she has at least placed some value on herself by rejecting the grotesque Mr Eccles.

The last we hear of her is when the new waiter at the Midnight Bell listens to her weeping in her room at half-past ten that night. What is the moral of the tale? The sheer sorrow of existence? That it is frightening and lonely to be alive?

Life was certainly bleak in Hamilton's eyes, and getting bleaker. At one point Ella looks out across traffic-choked London and thinks:

> It seemed as though some climax had just been reached, that civilisation was riding for a fall, that these days were certainly the last days of London, and that other dusks must soon gleam upon the broken chaos which must replace it.

Within a few years, the Second World War would commence, providing Hamilton with the perfect setting within which to explore his deepest fears.

3

Socialist Un-Realism: A Dystopian Journey

1935-39 More success: radio plays, stage hits and Marx. *Impromptu in Moribundia*

Following the completion of *Twenty Thousand Streets Under the Sky*, Hamilton admitted he felt "paralysed" with no new material to hand for a novel, having "used up all his experiences" thus far. Val Gielgud at the BBC then suggested he write another play, "a psychological thriller along the lines of *Rope* would be grand".

The result, *Money With Menaces* wasn't quite that but was a skilfully-crafted dramatic 'machine' with a simple plot. A rich businessman is blackmailed for money by someone who claims he has kidnapped his daughter. In the end, it turns out that the blackmailer is mainly concerned to wreak revenge for humiliations visited upon him by the businessman when they were at school together. It drew on Hamilton's experiences as a child at school, having suffered similar indignities to those of the blackmailer. The play was a success.

It would be another four years before he produced a novel. However, in the meantime, he found time to fall hopelessly in love with an actress, Geraldine Fitzgerald, and to make a rare trip across the Atlantic to visit New York and later to Barbados to stay with his brother. The journey simply revealed how much he hated travelling.

When his next novel did appear, in February 1939, it was utterly atypical of anything that had preceded it or what would follow. The book is a satirical fable in which a nameless narrator is transported by means of a device called the 'Asteradio' to a distant planet, Moribundia, an inverted vision or distorted mirror-image of 1930s Britain. It was perhaps inspired by a similar work of satirical science-fiction, *A Voyage to Puerilia*, written by the American novelist and expressionist playwright, Elmer Rice, in 1931. The book made clear Hamilton's hatred for aspects of English middle-class culture and consciousness. In the final analysis, it has been considered by many as a failure.

Underlying the various arguments concerning the worth or otherwise of this novel, however, is a struggle for Hamilton's posthumous political soul. His claims to being a Communist have been alternately belittled (by his brother, in particular) and defended (by various left-wing scholars and friends). The ultimate effect of his political views on his writing in general has also been challenged vigorously.

His brother wrote:

> Patrick had become, as theory went, a Marxist, and in the years that followed he accumulated a large library with the works of Marx, Lenin, and Stalin as its nucleus. There were indeed times when he could talk of little else. I must not exaggerate here for he was yet to produce some of his very best work in fiction and drama but I believe that the preoccupation did interfere with the work for which he was supremely gifted, and was in later years to contribute greatly to his troubles.

The radical journalist, Claud Cockburn, was scathing of this idea:

> It is characteristic I think that Bruce, even comprehending how a theory, a philosophy of life, could legitimately assume so dominant a role in a man's 'real' life and 'real' work as it did in the life and work of his brother, does not recognise that without that philosophy, without some agenda for the mastery of chaos, Patrick might well have degenerated into a mediocre man of undirected talent.

To his brother's later remark that Hamilton's Marxism was "simply a form of escape to some kind of male security", Cockburn retorted: "It has never explained just how a philosophy of endless change, endless struggle, endless search for solutions to endlessly evolving new confrontations could be considered any kind of escape to any kind of security."

In the pre-Second World War years, Hamilton certainly discussed the Soviet Union and Communism at great length with his brother, who travelled there in the late 1920s to investigate the evolving Stalinist state for himself. Hamilton, however, never joined the official Communist Party nor engaged in any significant political activities. He was simply not a 'joiner', as Claud Cockburn's abortive attempt to get him to write for the *Daily Worker* would ultimately demonstrate.

It is very easy to dismiss Patrick's 'conversion' to Marxism as a middle-class affectation. He was certainly isolated from, and lacked contact with, the "proletariat", as one commentator put it. He was solidly middle class and had grown up in a household with servants. As an almost instantly successful playwright, he had never had to work and never needed to write purely for money. Intellectually, he belonged, as the academic Brian McKenna has put it, to "that generation of English bourgeois intellectuals, born in the mid-1900s, who experienced the Great War at a close second hand, rebelled against their parents' generation in the Twenties, fell in love with the working class and the USSR in the Thirties, and sat out the Second World War on the Home Front."

It is certainly clear that he was of the view, as were so many others in the 1930s, that capitalism was reaching the end of its life. The chaos and cruelties of the Depression and the rise of Fascism indicated that something more humane must soon replace it. He also blindly refused to be swayed in the succeeding decades by the evidence pouring out of the Soviet Union of famines, mass trials, the secret police and political purges. Indeed, for some time he retained a dogged affection for Joe Stalin and dismissed the idea that the whole Marxist 'experiment' was a failure.

The biographer Michael Holroyd wrote of Hamilton's Marxism that it

> became a method of distinguishing between the avoidable and unavoidable suffering of people and, in so far as literature can change social conditions, such a vivid facsimile in fiction may have helped to do so. His Marxism is a sort of wish for a better social system that will bring less materially driven unhappiness. His Marxism was focussed on taking away the idea of inequality of wealth but he was aware that this would not end unhappiness – that's why his books have a streak of

tragedy running through them. People would still fall in love and get hurt.

For what it is worth, his personal politics were always somewhat idiosyncratic. In the 1950s, for example, he admitted that, whereas he had previously abstained from voting in general elections, he was now intending to vote Conservative. This was not, he insisted, an abandonment of his Marxist convictions but a "rational accommodation of changed circumstances". Now that the dream of Marxist socialism was "meaningless", he asserted, "I feel entirely justified in selfishly pursuing my own material and cultural interests. These, naturally, will be those of my own nation and my own nation is, I think, likely to be best served by the Tory Party." As for the working classes, he bemoaned the fact that they now, "hoisted TV masts instead of the Red Flag", and "had proved themselves despicably incapable of what might have been their historic task".

In mid-1938, Hamilton was busy writing his second stage hit, *Gaslight*, which borrowed a dramatic device from a story written earlier by his brother. In the days when houses were lit by gas, whenever someone entered or left, turning lights on and off, the gas flames already in use elsewhere in the house rose and fell accordingly. Thus, one was always aware of another's unseen movements. The plot involvs a man who brings his wife to live in a house where years earlier he had strangled another woman. He is searching for the jewels he missed at the time while simultaneously trying to convince his wife that she is going mad. It was, Hamilton said, "a Victorian thriller in three acts."

The play opened in December 1938 in Richmond and then transferred to the Apollo in the West End of London the following year for a run crowned by a visit from King George VI and Queen Elizabeth. It received near unanimous praise and was the event of the London theatrical season. After six months it transferred to Broadway in New York where it enjoyed a huge money-making success, running for four years. Eventually it became the longest-running foreign drama in Broadway history making Hamilton an even wealthier Marxist than he was already.

Which was just as well, because *Impromptu in Moribundia*, which appeared the following year, would earn him hardly a penny.

Impromptu in Moribundia

> *(Marxism) is not only my religion – it is my hobby. This thing means something to me. It is not a game – it is my vocation.*
>
> Patrick Hamilton

What sort of impact, if any, did Hamilton's political beliefs have on his writing? Can we say, as Brian McKenna does, that his Marxism "enabled him to conceptualise the condition of contemporary London as a metaphor for the crisis of capitalism in the early 1930s"? Or that, in Claud Cockburn's words, it rescued Patrick from, "degenerating into mediocrity" as a writer?

Discussion of *Impromptu in Moribundia*, his most experimental but least successful novel in commercial terms, is complicated by the fact that both of Hamilton's principal biographers and his brother have dismissed the book in different ways, considering it a "mistake", a misjudgement, "a failure" and "so misconceived, in general and in detail, as to be almost beyond criticism".

Yet there are those who consider that it merits favourable comparison with Aldous Huxley's *Brave New World* (1932) and George Orwell's *Nineteen Eighty-Four* (1948), and that it is a member of a generic family of satirical fables that also includes Jonathan Swift's *Gulliver's Travels* (1726) and *A Modest Proposal* (1729).

In brief, *Impromptu in Moribundia* is an imaginative, highly critical analysis of sleepy, small-minded English culture between the Wars during which the unnamed narrator travels across the country, has various enlightening experiences of Moribundian life before falling in love with a young girl called Anne. He is finally chased out of Moribundia by its enraged inhabitants for contravening certain social rules.

According to Brian McKenna, the novel firstly, "lays on the table Hamilton's conviction that in the stagnancy and stupidity of the English middle-class way of life resided the sickness of his society; and secondly because it employs an uncompromisingly fabulor mode to expose it."

In fact, *Impromptu* was only one of a flood of non-realist, yet non-modernist, socialist novels written in the 1930s.

Why had so many writers on the left turned away from straight realism? Possibly because many of the Left literary intelligentsia of the 1930s thought 'bourgeois' realism, as they termed it, was an inadequate tool with which to undertake the urgent task of social critique. They considered that traditional western education had managed to render the ordinary reader blind to the obvious iniquities and distortions of capitalism. Thus, to present an unadorned Marxist view of England at that time ran the risk of having the whole picture scornfully rejected. The wooden, two-dimensional 'socialist realism' literature beloved of Stalin's Cultural Commissar, Zhdanov, and his acolytes, with its hymns to hydro-electric dams and clean-living, hard-working heroes, was also clearly inadequate.

What was needed was a mode of delivery that could make a frontal assault on a class whose "gigantic temperamental dullness" was both a protection against the oblique thrust and the centre of the very malaise the novelist wished to expose. Allegory and fable might manage that task, their advantage over realism being that, using them, the writer could construct an argument upon its own terms of reference.

For instance, Hamilton clearly found the tactics of the resurgent advertising industry during the 1930s distasteful and potentially dangerous for the population as a whole. Thus he lampoons such techniques in Moribundia by taking them *literally*. Moribundian characters are made to extol the merits of particular commodities *in the very language of the adverts themselves*. What's more, he makes the Moribundians themselves become the physical manifestation of the ads. On the way to the shops with his guide, Anne, the narrator encounters a man with rheumatism tormented with lightning bolts of pain; a woman with a target on her nose and two arrows labelled "germs" and "infection"; a man with a dripping tap on his nose; and a young man suffering from indigestion, as signified by the little devils who prod his stomach with forks.

Thus Hamilton, in the words of Goldsmiths' College's Neil Maycroft, "indicts the ideology of capitalism by lampooning the rhetoric which encodes its advertising". Maycroft continues, "In this sense, the world of Moribundia can itself be seen as the commodity writ large. Today, consumption is promoted as a prime leisure activity in itself, as well as a way of marking social distinction. It is touted as an activity that promises physical, emotional and psychological satisfaction for all of our needs, both conscious and unconscious.

Moreover, the so-called 'politics' of consumption that revolve around the construction of 'identities' and 'lifestyles' attests to the centrality of consumption in the form of consumerism. While people today may not explicitly use the language of advertisements, they do often turn themselves into walking advertisements for capitalist enterprises through the wearing of all manner of conspicuous labels, brands and logos." In that sense, Hamilton's tale is prescient.

To achieve the estrangement from reality necessary to such a text, Hamilton uses various defamiliarizing effects. Systems of belief, names of places and individuals are reversed "msixram" for Marxism, "Ehtteivosnoinu" for the Soviet Union, "S.T. Toile" for T.S. Eliot, and so on. There is also the device called 'ballooning' whereby speech bubbles similar to those employed in comic books appear in the air around each character as they speak – except that, in Moribundia, the inhabitants can actually see and read them! In some conversations, a balloon appears out of the top of a Moribundian's head on which are inscribed the words of an advertisement of the 'Thinks' variety. These are physically depicted in the text in graphic typographical form.

Moribundia itself has just two classes – working and middle. The working class think and act exactly as the middle class likes to *believe* they think and act. Although materially well off, Moribundian workers keep coal in the bath, chop up grand pianos each week for firewood, and admit "We're hopeless. We don't even try. All we think of today is how we can avoid work – how we can scamp a job and get more money for it. There's not such a thing, any more, as honest pride in a job well done. We're thoroughly spoiled, that's what the matter is."

The middle class is represented by the 'little men', all identically diminutive, bowler-hatted and be-suited, the self-appointed guardians of the moral law of Moribundian society. Once again, Hamilton was drawing his material from contemporary Britain. A famous *Daily Express* political cartoonist of the 1930s, Sidney Strube, had created a 'Little Man' character, with his umbrella, bow-tie and bowler hat. The 'Little Man' became a national symbol of the long-suffering man-in-the-street, struggling, in Strube's own words, "with his everyday grumbles and problems, trying to keep his ear to the ground, his nose to the grindstone, his eye to the future and his chin up – all at the same time."

Whereas Strube saw his Little Man as admirable, for Hamilton he (and no doubt the newspaper in which he appeared) represented all that is "meanest, timidest, puniest, most conservative and insignificant" in society. He went further. The repugnant features of Hamilton's Little Men exemplified what he saw as the fascistic tendencies of the petty bourgeoisie. At the end of the book, a mob of these little men hounds the narrator out of Moribundia for contravening its small-minded, petty-bourgeois code and, he says:

> Instead of the harmless, helpless, friendly, tolerant, duty-doing little businessmen ... I saw cupidity, ignorance, complacence, meanness, ugliness, short-sightedness, cowardice, credulity, hysteria and, when the occasion called for it, ... cruelty and blood-thirstiness. I saw the shrewd and despicable cash basis underlying that idiotic patriotism, and a deathly fear and hatred of innovation.

In fact, at the time of its original publication, *Impromptu* wasn't considered anything like as bad as his biographers think it now. Lettice Cooper in *Time and Tide* commented, "In fact this is a good Marxist pamphlet in a light and readable form." The *New Statesman* praised it highly: "Mr. Hamilton, wisely choosing a well-defined target, hits with precision and *Impromptu in Moribundia* is not only extremely amusing but an excellent piece of satire."

Unfortunately, *Moribundia* appeared at an inconvenient point in history. A year after its publication, Germany turned its guns on the Soviet Union and the latter found itself standing shoulder to shoulder with the capitalist west. Stalin suddenly needed to ingratiate himself and his regime with the sorts of people socialists like Hamilton had been savaging! What's more, 'Unchange', a key characteristic of Moribundian society and thus held up to ridicule by Hamilton, suddenly seemed attractive to a British nation struggling to preserve what appeared to be enduring values based on the virtues of the 'unchanging' English countryside, its history and traditions.

Dad's Army's Captain Mainwaring, a bowler-hatted character who would appear perfectly at home in Moribundia or in the cartoons of Strube, remains today a hero rather than a villain. His characteristic mix of pomposity and snobbery seem only to make him endearing rather than hateful. Meanwhile, the virtues of suburbia, spiritual home of the conformist and the conservative, forever resurface to be celebrated anew. John Betjeman was a great fan of Hamilton's, but while Betjeman's poetry is informed by an underlying social critique, it is laced with great yearning for the lost innocence of MetroLand, home of the bowler-hats. It could also be asked, didn't the members of the exploitative, degenerate elite satirised by Hamilton, not to mention the proletariat in cringing servitude to it, nonetheless somehow manage to show extraordinary initiative, altruism, endurance and, in many cases, even heroism during the war about to engulf them?

Fundamentally, what is missing from *Impromptu*, however, is what draws the majority of readers to Hamilton's work, and which sorely disappoints with its absence. Hamilton biographer Sean French says, "Throughout *Moribundia*, Hamilton deprives himself of his greatest gift, which is his eye for what life is like beneath people's facile illusions and myths. He is a master of the particular who has shackled himself to a story about generalities."

Unlike similar forays into the dystopian fable such as Orwell's *Nineteen Eighty-Four* and Huxley's *Brave New World*, no strong central character emerges in *Impromptu* for readers to empathise with – either to love or hate or laugh at. One of the major strengths of a Hamilton novel is that it will contain strong and memorable characters. From Bob, Ella and Jenny in *Twenty Thousand Streets under the Sky*, to Netta Longdon and George Henry Bone in *Hangover Square*, to Miss Roach and Mr Thwaites in *The Slaves of Solitude*, right through to the monster, Gorse, in the trilogy that bears his name, it's the chilling, touching, sometimes maddening reality of the human creations through which he tells his stories, that captivates and enthrals us.

Even such an enthusiastic apologist for the book such as Peter Widdowson, who oversaw the re-publication of *Impromptu* in 1999, sensed certain misgivings, that this style of writing was not Hamilton's forte: He concluded, " ... for the novelist with a strong sense of the rich specificity of social behaviour, it is exactly here that the disadvantage of the dystopic fable lies. Will the satire stick?" The answer is probably no.

Impromptu in Moribundia would be the first and last time Hamilton would stray from his established narrative style and methodology. Within two years he would produce possibly his finest novel, about which there would be no disagreements, ideological or otherwise, amongst his critical admirers.

4

Finest Hours: The Home Front

1939-1947 War service, a West End hit, peacetime and drink.
Hangover Square, The Slaves of Solitude

At the beginning of the Second World War, Hamilton and his wife were living in a flat in Henley-on-Thames in Surrey although he also had a London base in a superior guest house near Sloane Square. This was necessary both for his social forays into the West End of London and also useful when he took a short-lived job on *Time and Tide* magazine as a theatre reviewer.

Like many of his left-leaning friends, Hamilton was invigorated by the sense that he was living in the last days of the existing, outmoded society and was anxious for the war to sweep it all away. He wrote to his brother Bruce: "I always knew that the Second World War would be the end of life as we knew it and, alas, I still think so. But a better world will come out of it all right and if you and I aren't starved or bumped off by some explosive, we'll live to see it ... "

Like so many cynics, however, he became increasingly bemused when the bombing failed to have the terrible impact on day-to-day life he'd expected:

> ... it is astonishing how quickly the town pulls round and establishes a new modus vivendi in a few days. People of course are 'wonderful'. What one can put up with when one has to.

His underlying loyalties to England and its characteristic virtues surfaced, despite his best intentions. These would gradually be reflected in his fiction. In many ways, he had little to complain about as the conflict progressed. Indeed, he would have a 'good war'. Now 37 and categorised as a non-combatant, military service of some kind beckoned. In the event, he eventually pulled strings and got a job with Entertainments National Service Association (ENSA) writing linking material for various variety acts. Otherwise, *Gaslight* was making him, as he put it, "an astounding amount of money". His books were being read, his plays were on stage and radio ... ("the BBC never put on anything else!"). Even *Craven House* was reissued in 1942 with some minor edits.

Sexually and socially, he was certainly having a good time. According to his brother Bruce, he "attained maturity in his sex life during the war ... with tarts, not very frequently and usually when tight." With such women he was able to engage in the milder forms of masochism he reputedly enjoyed, evidence for which came from the memoirs of Claud Cockburn whom he met at this time and who was soon one of his principal drinking companions.

According to brother Bruce:

> Under the combined influence of alcohol and Claud's close companionship, Patrick confided many of his most closely guarded secrets – particularly those to do with sex. He would tell Coburn that he frequented prostitutes – particularly those who had no objection to indulging his penchant for enacting his domination fantasies, tying them up preparatory to engaging in various sado-masochistic games and rituals. Patrick attributed this behaviour in part to the fact that he felt he was too ugly, especially after his accident, to attract anyone other than prostitutes.

As ever, work continued apace. On New Year's Eve, 1940, Hamilton announced to Bruce that he had started a "thriller", a "Blitzy novel" called *Hangover Square*. The book did not arrive without a struggle however. After an enthusiastic start, by 1941 the exhilaration of war was wearing off to be replaced by, as he wrote to his brother, "the bloody inconvenience and the boredom – the restrictions, the blackout, the travelling, petrol, parking and telephone difficulties." This impacted on his writing. He had to force himself to stay in bed all day and write. But by this time he was drinking a great deal of whiskey in the evenings. When he finished the book in March that year, however, he confided in Bruce that, "I have the feeling that it's the best thing I've ever written."

Set in 1938 in the grimy publands of Earls Court, *Hangover Square*'s protagonist, semi-alcoholic George Harvey Bone, falls hopelessly in love with Netta Longdon, a callous, small-time London actress. In many respects, the novel is a more distressing reworking of Bob's suffering in *The Midnight Bell* as Netta strings Bone along, leeching his cash and his dignity until he can take no more. Unlike Bob, however, Bone cannot run away to sea and the novel ends in cathartic violence.

Netta, however, is a more fully-realised femme fatale 'bitch' than Jenny and soon became the focus of many book reviewers' attention. James Agate in the *Daily Express* enthused: "This magnificent thriller is the best study of a trull since Shakespeare's Cressida … Don't gulp this. Ration yourself to 50 pages a day and make it last a week." The book was an instant commercial success.

Once he had finished *Hangover Square*, he set about writing another play for the West End and in 1942, *The Duke In Darkness* appeared. This was an historical melodrama set in the latter part of the 16th century about an imaginary imprisoned French duke. It ran for two months but did not enjoy the success of *Gaslight* or *Rope* for it lacked their sheer tension. It contained an optimistic political message, however, as it allegorized national liberation with particular reference to the Nazi occupation of France. Hamilton managed to paraphrase part of one of Lenin's tracts, 'One Step Forward, Two Steps Back' and put the words into the mouth of the duke as he escapes to raise a rebellion among his supporters:

> And then the people will be the world, and the world all the people – and the world will be its fair self, not the wild arena of slaughter, devilry and misery it is now.

Soon after this, he began his next novel, *The Slaves of Solitude*, but found the going extremely tough. He put it aside and instead turned to yet another play, *The Governess*, which ultimately failed to appear in the West End for contractual reasons.

Along with the rest of the country, Hamilton greeted victory over Germany with mixed feelings, writing to his brother that he was both relieved and mentally exhausted.

The struggle to finish *Slaves* resumed. He returned to Henley and wrote steadily each day until five or six o'clock when he allowed himself the necessary luxury of his daily drink. It was finally finished in 1946 and appeared in print in 1947.

It is the tale of a unmarried professional woman who flees the Blitz seeking solitude in a boarding house on the outskirts of London, only to find herself embroiled in a tortuous battle of wills with some of the other co-inhabitants. It was instantly acclaimed and considered generally to be his masterpiece. Nevertheless, it marked the beginning of the end of his literary career, due in large part to his increasing alcohol addiction. Ironically, his brother Bruce commented on reading the book, "This novel ... was saturated, almost drowned in drink; the governing condition of its little world."

Hangover Square

> *Bone is quite a creation – and I'm not sure it's not my best.*
> Patrick Hamilton

Taking place between Christmas Day 1938 and 4th September 1939, when war was declared, *Hangover Square* tells of George Harvey Bone's desperate and ultimately tragic pursuit of a wilfully unpleasant aspiring actress called Netta Longdon. Netta is shallow, desirable, but contemptuous of George and and well beyond his reach. She toys with him just so as long as he has money with which to indulge her sordid behaviour. At the same time, she and her friends subject him to a sadistic regime of systematic humiliation and insult – a dangerous game, as George is clearly mentally unwell. He suffers from a strange condition that come and goes without warning. When thinking rationally, he is a pathetic, weak-willed character, given to heavy bouts of drinking and seemingly unable to break clear of his obsession with Netta. When suffering from his strange moods, however, he is another person entirely, driven solely by a compulsion to kill Netta. His rational self is never able to remember what his 'somnambulistic' self is telling him to do, and so we watch as he unconsciously moves towards his goal. By telling the reader what Bone is ultimately going to do, but depriving the character himself of such knowledge, we are hypnotically drawn into the pursuit, appalled at Netta's behaviour but, rather like children at a pantomime, thrilled at the fact that she cannot see the monster looming just behind her.

Hangover Square is considered by many to be one of his finest novels, putting him in the same bracket as Christopher Isherwood, F. Scott Fitzgerald and Graham Greene, as a novelist who creates myths of social decay out of an individual crisis. The book has been particularly likened in form and spirit, by Professor Peter Widdowson, to George Orwell's *Coming Up For Air*, which came out in 1939. Widdowson notes, "Both books demonstrate a concern for the same things: the meaning of the oncoming war for the common man and woman, and the way in which the growing alienation of the modern world was part and parcel of the violence to come."

Coming Up For Air records a man's failed attempt to run away to the security of his childhood. George Bowling is unhappy with his expanding waist and receding hairline, not to mention his menial job. He is also unhappy with the world at large and fears the war that seems to be inevitably on the horizon. He therefore makes the ill-fated decision to return to the town where he grew up, where he finds the fields in which he played paved over and the pond in which he fished filled in. What's more, his childhood sweetheart is just as physically out-of-condition as George himself!

Orwell has written of the book: "Through Bowling I was able to give vent to my own anxieties, which I think reflected the anxieties of the whole nation – that is, the escalating violence, cruelty and destruction typical of the 20th century. I placed the book in a familiar setting deliberately to drive home the point of people going about everyday life with outward calmness but with inner feelings of trepidation and doubt."

Hamilton, too, uses his character to dramatize certain of his own feelings, but whereas in *Coming Up For Air,* the onset of a war is examined and explained in concrete political images, in *Hangover Square* the conflict is more patently *felt* and *feared.*

Sean French saw the book as "a near-expressionist version of Hamilton's own fear ... whose most realistic aspects are those where the world had changed to fit the author's already existing paranoia." The reference to Expressionism is intriguing.

He may well have been drawing on his close study of Nietzsche when arranging the elements of his tale. In *The Birth of Tragedy*, Nietzsche presents his theory of the ancient dualism between two types of aesthetic experience, namely the Apollonian and the Dionysian; a dualism between a world of the mind, of order, of regularity and polishedness and a world of intoxication, chaos, ecstasy. According to Nietzsche, both elements are present in any work of art.

The basic characteristics of Expressionism are Dionysian: bold colours, distorted forms, painted in a careless manner, two-dimensional, without perspective, and based on the feelings of a child rather than on adult rational thought. In *Hangover Square*, Hamilton's subjective expression of inner experience is emphasised; inner feelings are expressed through a distorted rendition of reality made concrete by Bone's strange mental disorder. Bone himself describes what it is like when the mood descends upon him:

> A silent film without music – he could have found no better way of describing the weird world in which he now moved. He looked at passing objects and people, but they had no colour, vivacity, meaning – he was mentally deaf to them. They moved like automatons, without motive, without volition of their own ... They had no valid existence; they were not creatures experiencing pleasure or pain. There was, in fact, no sensation, no pleasure or pain at all in this world: there was only himself – his dreary, numbed, dead self.

Ill-at-ease, a lonely, unrelated figure whose values (like Orwell's George) are those of a lost Edwardian past, an idyllic, pre-war world of childhood, Bone is unhinged by the faint but insistent rumble of the coming war. While he feels uninvolved with the issues surrounding the war, at the same time he can't help feeling a sense of 'disgrace' about a Munich settlement that seemed to rubber-stamp the appeasement of Hitler. There was, Bone thought, something *indecent* about it, particularly as Peter and Netta set out on a drinking binge to celebrate it. Thus a definite relationship is established between George's private tragedy and the enormous tragedy of Europe.

A great deal of critical attention has been focused on the

significance of its secondary characters, Netta and Peter. Biographer Nigel Jones considered the book a major advance over *Twenty Thousand Streets* because, "where Jenny and Mr Eccles were laughably loathsome in themselves (they) were no physical threat to anyone. Peter and Netta are in another league entirely; despicable, certainly, but also deeply dangerous because *the attitudes they represent* have already undermined and threaten to overturn what Hamilton understood as the civilised decencies of life: democracy, culture and common humanity."

Netta and Peter, her boyfriend, clearly represent what Hamilton and many more on the left saw as the real enemy – the petty bourgeoisie in its final attempt to preserve its power against the inevitable triumph of socialism and the working class. Novelist and critic D.J. Taylor says of *Hangover Square*: "Hamilton saw the psychological roots of fascism", while Brian McKenna regards the depiction of Peter, in particular, as a "perfect dissection of the psychology of fascism". With his "nasty fair hair, with his nasty fair guardsman's moustache, along with his clothes, his habitual grey check trousers and polo-neck sweaters which Hamilton decided served the function of a uniform", Peter was, "a scornful, ultra-masculine man who desired to single himself out from the herd ..." Meanwhile, the writer Christopher Hitchens recently went as far as to compare the Führer-adoring, Mosley-marrying Diana Mitford to Netta.

Hamilton's skill at realising such a character produced, according to Claud Cockburn, a comical situation which for a time was embarrassing:

> The head of the Cultural Division of the British Communist Party told me that the party chiefs were worried because I was seeing so much of Hamilton and, they said, there were strong grounds for believing that Patrick had Fascist connections – that he was perhaps an agent. Questioning him I found that the ground for this strange belief was that the villain in one of Patrick's earlier novels, *Hangover Square*, was a Fascist. 'So what?' I asked. The cultural communist said that it was the general opinion of the Comrades that nobody could possibly reproduce exactly the manners, speech, outlook, and behaviour of a Fascist who had not been or did

not have the most intimate connections with the Blackshirts. It took a number of uproarious and deeply sympathetic meetings between myself, Patrick, and several party leaders to convince them that Fascism for Patrick was the embodiment of all that he most hated.

Ironically, given Hamilton's disdain for the Bloomsbury set, it's been suggested by literary scholar and critic Bernard Bergonzi, that *Hangover Square* was a novel of "traditional physical and psychological realism" sharing with Virginia Woolf's *Between The Acts* "a strong evocation of the last days of a doomed peace. It documented the sense of the ending of an age." Woolf's novel, of course, was trying to uncover the roots of Fascism in Great Britain, seeking to find it in the English Pageant.

Tellingly, Netta, according to the narrative, "was supposed to dislike Fascism, to laugh at it, but actually she liked it enormously. In secret she liked pictures of marching, regimented men, in secret she was physically attracted to Hitler; she did not really think that Mussolini looked like a funny burglar. She liked the uniforms, the guns, the breeches, the boots, the swastikas, the shirts. She was probably sexually stimulated by these things in the same way as she might have been sexually stimulated by a bull-fight ... It might be said that this feeling for violence and brutality, for a pageant and panorama of fascism on the continent, formed her principal disinterested aesthetic pleasure."

Thus Woolf and Hamilton appear to share a desire to seek the fascist lurking within the English middle-class psyche, seeing fascism not as something 'foreign' but as a peculiarly class phenomenon.

Not everyone agrees that the novel can be fitted into a political 'frame', however. Poet and academic, Leo Mellor, feels that this sort of analysis fails, "because readers leave the novels with no grand sense of explanation, or even of how these characters fit into history at a certain point."

J.B. Priestley agrees, feeling that it wasn't Marxism but an abhorrence of modern urban life generally that animated Hamilton. Many people on both the left and the right of politics felt that the interwar years were a "low, dishonest decade" and Hamilton, Priestley suggests, felt his half-mad character was the one to bring it all crashing down.

Professor Robert Hewison felt that the book exuded "nihilism mixed with despair and disillusion, an aimless post-Munich world of public houses and wasted time" and quoted Bone on hearing that war was imminent:

> What if there was a war? Yes – if nothing else turned up, a war might. A filthy idea but what if a war was what he was waiting for? That might put a stop to it all. They might get him – he might be conscripted away from drinks and smokes and Netta. At times he could find it in his heart to hope for a war – bloody business as it all was.

If *Hangover Square* had been a product of Russian Socialist Realism (Maxim rather than Arshile Gorky) then we might have expected Bone, representing the anti-Fascist mind, to be killing the Fascists *because* they were Fascists. But that's not the case. Bone himself has hardly any philosophical/political convictions – just a sense of foreboding and dread at what is coming, mingled with a certain ill-defined shame. He really doesn't *know* why he's supposed to be killing them. The besotted sot would apparently have been perfectly happy to have possessed Netta, political warts and all, had she decided to love or pity or even marry him. He was certainly overjoyed when, towards the end of the book, she agreed to go to Brighton with him. It was all he really desired.

Perhaps it's what really propels *Hangover Square*: the predicament of a hurt and defenceless man who desperately desires to be loved. George Harvey Bone appears to us as tragic because his plight is, despite its extreme nature, somehow universal: we can recognise in him our own poor judgments in both friends and desire.

Which brings us to that strange psychological device, the dual world into which he suddenly snaps without warning. According to Marxist scholar John Mepham: "The novel is stylistically interesting in the rendering of George's odd inner life. His split personality, which swings between impotent passivity and violent revenge, creates a powerfully surreal atmosphere."

Sean French, however, suggests the "clumsy, unnecessary and unconvincing device of George's split personality, a literary mechanism rather than a medical condition … fudges the crucial moral and aesthetic challenge of the book, which is to justify the final terrible murder at the end."

In fact, the murders could seem unnecessary in many ways, for there had already been an 'ending' of sorts. Bone thinks that Netta has succeeded in using him to the extent that she has ingratiated herself with his oldest and best friend (who represented all the good things he yearned for) and that she has managed to infiltrate herself with Eddie, a theatrical producer for whom Bone worked occasionally. Bone finds himself drunk and distraught in Brighton, all alone, and it seems that he may even kill himself.

But, almost in 'country dance style', his friend finds him and ushers him into the theatre where Bone finds himself with all the good, important people in his life who treat him well and more or less tell him that Netta was a 'bitch' after all. They sweep him up and take him along in Eddie's large, beautiful car and he finds himself 'in' with a male 'in-crowd'. Netta is thus banished, dismissed in male chauvinistic terms.

Such a redemptive finale might have solved Bone's problems. Instead, Hamilton invokes the mysterious SNAP! and suddenly George is hell-bent on murder again, which he duly carries out before heading (still in this weird but now permanent state) for Maidenhead, which he finds empty and depressing. He then kills himself. The tiny tragedy of Bone's demise is deliberately made to read like pulp fiction, in a sense, and the report of his death, forced off the front page by the breaking out of war, is likewise reduced to a tabloid headline.

SLAYS TWO
FOUND GASSED
Thinks of cat

Hamilton mentions in a letter to his brother that criminal-maniacs are "sorts of somnambulists. They live in a sort of dream – an evil dream." If Bone's strange state is this 'somnambulism' referred to as characteristic of murderers, then Bone's no socialist avenger – he's simply a killer. Likewise, if Bone is merely ill, then are we just watching a sick person going about murder? If not, what can his 'schizophrenia' *mean*? Is it a symbol for something else?

Goldsmiths' College's Neil Maycroft has sought to link the condition with what he terms the "technique of 'inversion'" used in

Impromptu in Moribundia that is used to reflect back to us a society organised along the lines of capitalist and bourgeois ideology made concrete:

> This theme of inversion finds a more subtle yet also more powerful expression in Hamilton's later novel, *Hangover Square* (1941). Using a contrivance whereby the book's central character is suffering from a form of schizophrenia, Hamilton produces a series of contrasting inversions of the world around him. The ability of the character to distinguish what is real and what is an illusion, caused by attacks of his 'dead moods', becomes progressively less certain, until the 'alienated' view of the world eventually becomes the rationally accepted one that disastrously guides the character's actions.

For some, the murder of Netta causes unease. According to Dr Brian McKenna, many critics, male and female, call her a "bitch" which he feels "evidences the profundity of the splenetic outrage engendered by Hamilton's virago. She is able to function like this by virtue of the way she is constructed as a catalyst for powerfully contradictory emotions." McKenna feels that Hamilton clearly hates the various femme fatales that figure in his work. Miss Cotterill, Jenny, and later Vicki Kugelmann, all are described as "indifferent", "apathetic", and "unmoved" which, according to McKenna, signifies the worst in Hamilton. "Indifferent" in particular is "an ethically heavily freighted term in the Hamiltonian scheme of things. The hallmark of his evil characters – conducive to fascism."

Netta is the greatest femme fatale figure in his literature and Hamilton, according to McKenna, is clearly on Bone's side against her. "The main psychological account of Netta's character is weighted with all the authority typical of the ultra-reliable, extra-diegetic narrator."

Extradiegetic narrators are those who have a connection to the 'public' in the way that they address their story to a reader who exists outside of their own story. Narrators are defined by narrative distance: that is, by the amount of knowledge they have about the events they are narrating. Since possessing knowledge inevitably affects power relationships, narrative distance is a key factor in inclusion and exclusion. We, the readers, are clearly included in the club that hates Netta. Early in the novel she is described thus:

> Her thoughts, however, resembled those of a fish – something seen floating in a tank, brooding, self-absorbed, frigid, moving solemnly forward to its object or veering slowly sideways without fully conscious motivation ... Spoiled from the earliest days because of her physical beauty: made a fuss of, given in to, blest with favours, the fulfilment of her desires going ahead at roughly the same pace as their conception, she had become totally impassive: thought and action were atrophied.

Bone couldn't think all the things placed inside his brain, thus they must be Hamilton talking. From start to finish, therefore, the narrative tends to enlist the reader uncritically against "wicked old Netta" and *alongside* the "battered bruiser", George. McKenna asks – how is the reader manipulated into *wanting* Netta killed? Principally via those strange 'dead' moods and Bone's prevarication within them. There is the repetition of phrases concerning "putting it off" and the way he keeps on forgetting what it is he has to do. We, the readers don't forget, however, and so we become, according to McKenna, like children at a pantomime screaming "that's what you must do!"

McKenna thus feels that "the construction of Netta tends to produce misogynistic effects" which somewhat spoils the effect of Hamilton's "anti-Fascist radicality". It is necessary, he feels, "to defuse this explosive misogyny", principally because the portrait of Netta is "a radical exposure of middle-class philistinism as cognate with a passive support for fascism". By making her such a Fascist-lover, Hamilton "gets away with" justifying (in fictional terms) her murder which McKenna thinks is vile: put simply, Hamilton links her with Fascists so as to feel happy about engineering her death – but the real reason for having her killed is he hates her because of her sexuality. McKenna and others have asked, if Netta were as indifferent to the blandishments of Fascism as she is to the overtures of Bone, Hamilton would have had difficulty with "getting away with" his woman-hating portrait and in justifying it to his own conscience ..." McKenna asks, "Why *can't* Netta say she doesn't want to go out with him? If all women were murdered for saying no to a man, there wouldn't be a woman alive."

Only, she doesn't do any such simple thing as just saying no. She torments, manipulates and uses Bone, sleeps with her boyfriend under his very nose and drops him the moment his usefulness wanes. She really does behave in a most disgusting way.

Thus, it might not be her 'Fascism' that convinces us her murder is 'justified' – if we actually do think that. That she is killed – a rare, indeed unique occurrence in a Hamilton novel – can certainly be justified in fictional terms. We know it is coming, but maybe we don't want it to happen. Who can speak for every reader? Her politics, to this reader, seem an affectation. A stance.

Bone certainly isn't a political thinker and yet some have even implicated him in the catastrophe that engulfed the world in 1939! Peter Widdowson goes so far as to suggest that George is as *organically responsible* for his own society as Netta and Peter are – his passivity, his indulgence, his abdication of responsibility fundamentally engender theirs. McKenna, too, sees Bone as complicit, principally because Bone's dislike of Peter stems from the latter's having 'done time' for assaulting an opponent – not because of his political violence. There's something 'common' about the man, in other words.

In terms of creating a fictional world, *Hangover Square* is a perfect example of Hamilton's magical ability to render place with compelling accuracy and style. The novel's greatest strength resides in that solid sense of a sordid, futile and irresponsible world, which is conveyed, according to Peter Widdowson, "as much by the cheap hotels, corner-houses, cinemas, pubs and streets, as by the sleazy self-indulgence of the characters and the drink-sodden atmosphere." Other critics have commented on this characteristic Hamiltonian touch.

Nick Hornby has written, "Hamilton ... is a sort of urban Thomas Hardy: he is always a pleasure to read, and as social historian he is unparalleled." And Doris Lessing has observed, "Hamilton is a social historian virtually without equal in his punctilious reckoning up of the minutiae of desperate lives in the interwar years. Now people have forgotten the kind of smell that came out of England in the 1930s." She says, "the cheese-paring and the obsession with money. Then, people were always calculating ... could they afford to have this drink here, or a cheaper meal there? A raffish world of rent arrears and post-dated cheques. Never has anyone written about crooks as well as Hamilton. And it's the details that are so absorbing."

In Hamilton's next novel, those 'absorbing details' would be marshalled to delineate the war that now engulfed both his real and his fictional worlds.

The Slaves of Solitude

> It is Hamilton's attempt to make a connection between large historical forces, the evil that we read about in the newspapers, and the squabbles and petty struggles that make up everyday individual experience.
>
> Sean French

Hangover Square ends as the war begins. During this time, Hamilton lived in Henley-on-Thames, a small town outside London, the population of which rose from 7,000 to 17,000 as people moved out of the city to escape the bombs. And it is in a fictionalised version of Henley (Thames Lockdon) that Hamilton sets his next, and most impressive, semi-comic novel, *The Slaves of Solitude*.

As in Hamilton's other novels, the plot itself is relatively simple. One of its greatest strengths is the focus on the creeping plight of the civilian population as the war takes its ghastly toll. Munton, writing on English Fiction of the Second World War, considers the book "the outstanding novel of non-combatant experience focussing as it does on the insidious side-effects of the conflict on the marginal civilian population."

The war appears alongside the other main characters as another personality. A growling, grim presence, infecting and darkening the lives of those whom it holds as slaves in thrall, "Like the devil in a morality play", according to Claude Cockburn. Hamilton captures perfectly the way the conflict gradually denudes everyone of items of ordinary usage – cigarettes from the tobacconists, sweets from the confectioners, pens and envelopes from the stationers, fittings from the hardware store.

"The war," he says, "which had begun by making dramatic and drastic demands, which had held up the public in style like a highwayman, had now developed into a petty pilferer, incessantly pilfering. You never knew where you were with it and you could not look round without finding something else gone or going."

Miss Roach, the book's unlikely heroine, is a single woman in her thirties who works for a City publishing company and returns every night from her work to her boarding house, The Rosamund Tea Rooms, in Thames Lockdon. She is one of a group of genteel evacuees who have the financial means to rent a room for the duration of the war and thus attempt to escape the horrors of the Blitz. Miss Roach is unusual in that she actually has a job and seems somehow more rooted in the here and now than the other, much older inhabitants of the Tea Rooms. They, by contrast, live in a strange, almost airless world, their lives measured-out by mealtimes, flavoured with inconsequential conversation.

The narrative explains:

> This system of separate tables, well meant as it may have been, added yet another hellish touch to the hellish melancholy prevailing. For, in the small space of the room, a word could not be uttered, a little cough could not be made, a hair-pin could not be dropped at one table without being heard at all the others; and the general self-consciousness which this caused smote the room with a silence, a conversational torpor, and finally a complete apathy from which it could not stir itself...

Life in The Rosamund Tea Rooms turns out to be a repetition of life in London with a vengeance – as the sense of imprisonment replaces the terrors of the blitz.

The lodgers, though privileged, have merely exchanged one kind of hell for another. Miss Roach, in particular, as we are positioned squarely on her shoulders, certainly endures great mental stresses and strains. Having exchanged an Anderson shelter for a proper upstairs bedroom, she finds she still cannot escape her anguished insomnia. Several long sections of the novel are devoted to her lonely sleeplessness caused: not simply by her fears of the conflict without but she is also obsessively trying to divine what her fellow lodgers' intentions towards her are. In many ways, it's simply another battle, but this time raging within the Tea Rooms, and within herself.

It is in the language of the Tea Rooms' inhabitants that the ultimate horror of Roach's situation is illustrated. Academic and critic, Thierry Labica, has examined the way in which the dry, lifeless speech of the boarding house is remorselessly explored by Hamilton: the routine questions and stock responses, the dread of revealing too much.

Labica explains, "In Hamilton's novels, verbal exchanges are often systematically evoked in terms of military tactics, at best tactical moves and at worst straightforward aggressions. Thus, Miss Roach spends a considerable amount of time wondering what other lodgers, Thwaites in particular, actually *meant* when they said what they said. And she does so to a point of ever greater insomnia."

Mr Thwaites, the other main character, often dominates the room by means of sheer vocal power; his "booming voice" reminding one of bombs going boom in central London; his utterances even seeming to mingle with food:

> And because Mr Thwaites said no more, the atmosphere in which pins could be heard dropping returned to the room, and no one else dared to say any more. Ruminatively, dully, around the heavy thoughts set in motion by Mr Thwaites, the heavy steamed pudding was eaten.

Thwaites is a spiteful, malevolent yet comically bizarre creation, an old bully who delights in torturing everything from flies to humans and even the very language he speaks. Yet another character based in part on Hamilton's father, he mimics others badly and unpredictably and with no sense of coherence or accuracy whatsoever. ("'As the Scotchman said,' said Mr Thwaites. 'Yes … I Hay ma Doots, as the Scotchman said – of Yore … '"). Thwaites spends so much time mangling the *way* something is said, he thus avoids *the substance* of what is being said. Towards the end of the book, during the final climactic argument, in the space of just one page, Miss Roach demands of him, "Will you please tell me what you mean?" no less than seven times! No wonder she sometimes feels she is losing her mind …

Nonetheless, because it is war-time, Miss Roach finds herself getting up to things, such as drinking by herself in the pub, that she would not normally have contemplated. Crucially, she even has an ambiguous but ultimately ungratifying affair with an amiable, inconsequential American officer of about her own age. Lieutenant Pike claims to own a laundry in Wilkes Barre, Pennsylvania and even proposes to her. She is tempted to accept though she does not love him; but then discovers that he proposes to practically every woman he meets.

The major plot line, however, concerns the way she is (or allows herself to be) driven to extremes of passionate hatred by Mr Thwaites, and Miss Vicki Kugelmann. Kugelmann is a German refugee who is at first excluded but, mainly via Miss Roach's kindliness, is then admitted to the Tea Rooms – only to turn on Miss Roach, expropriate her boyfriend and oppress her with her own verbal absurdities. Vicki's character is unreal, pure semblance reliant on a collage of set phrases and clichéd attitudes borrowed from old films and magazines.

Thwaites exploits what he sees as a possible rift between the two women where a man is concerned, and makes a point of contrasting Vicki's sexual allure with Miss Roach's aging wrinkles and maidenly plainness. The combination of Thwaites' inane stupidities and the spiteful, catty barbs of Kugelmann, reduces Miss Roach to a nervous wreck. Although portrayed initially by Hamilton as something of a repressed blue-stocking, it's ultimately her deeply maternal feelings for a teenager she befriends and which are wilfully misinterpreted and then turned into something 'filthy' by Thwaites and Kugelmann that finally breaks her resolve not to react. Outraged, she resorts to the 'female' tactic of pushing the ridiculous Thwaites and thus (indirectly) causes his death.

Both Thwaites and Kugelmann have qualities and predilections that reveal them as possible Nazis. Thus, a similar pattern is set to *Hangover Square*, where Netta and Peter – Fascists in spirit, possibly in fact – oppress and torment Bone until he cracks.

Like Netta Longdon, Thwaites is precisely unfeeling, indifferent, insouciant – features which Hamilton saw as enabling what Claud Cockburn called, "the terrible natural Naziness existing in all of us." In fact, his verbal aggression towards Miss Roach, whom he dislikes anyway, is inspired in part because he suspects she supports the Russians. Their victories were greeted with concealed dismay by those like Thwaites who secretly hoped the Germans wouldn't be defeated.

The fourth important character plays a much smaller but intriguing part in the development of the plot as it reaches its finale. Archie Prest is an enigmatic and very private Tea Rooms inhabitant. Gradually, we learn that he is an unemployed veteran variety performer who makes secret trips into London to keep in touch with his theatrical colleagues. Eventually, he gets work in a children's pantomime. Miss Roach discovers this towards the end of the book. They chat in a pub and he invites her to one of his shows. As she prepares finally to leave the Tea Rooms and return to London, she remembers the invitation. She goes and watches as Prest triumphs on stage at Wimbledon and, "Somehow his triumph seemed to be Miss Roach's triumph as well, and her heart lifted up with pleasure."

Stylistically, the novel is a return to more traditional methods after the experiment of *Impromptu In Moribundia*. We see the use of an intrusive and very judgemental narrator who becomes more and more prominent in Hamilton's later books. Miss Roach is continually hemmed in by the narrator's rendition of her internal thoughts although this works well in ways that recall the sharp insights of Jane Austen or George Eliot:

> "But, my dear, this is marvellous!" said Miss Roach, that slight film coming over her eyes which comes over the eyes of those who, while proclaiming intense pleasure, are actually thinking fast.

Where the 'politics' of the novel are concerned, Miss Roach undergoes something of a transformation. Initially, her attitude to the wider conflict is one of ostrich-like indifference. "If you could do nothing to alleviate a situation, what sense was there in thinking about it, talking about it, taking any interest in it?" Of an introvertedly anxious disposition, she watches a newsreel of the fighting and experiences, "fear of life, of herself, of Mr Thwaites, of the times and things into which she had been born." Thus, she is no political thinker. However, the personal gradually does become political as her animosity develops towards her two tormentors.

At one point Kugelmann voices the hope that, after the war is over, all decent people will understand "my poor Germany". Miss Roach ponders on what this means exactly. That it was only through a lack of "understanding" that the war had come about? That Nazi Germany was as much "in the right" as her opponents? Later in the book, the issue erupts again, and is the cause of Miss Roach finally turning on both Kugelmann and Thwaites. Kugelmann suggests that the whole issue of the war is "complicated" but Miss Roach insists it is very simple. "It's a simple conflict between all that's decent and all that's evil – and it's simple, that's all …"

When Miss Kugelmann responds by suggesting that Miss Roach has a simple mind, and follows this up with the jibe that she is just an insular Englishwoman and not "cosmopolitan" enough to grasp the "complications", Miss Roach has had enough. Does being "cosmopolitan in outlook," she demands, "mean that you think things are so complicated that you support the Nazis in all the murder and filth and torture they've been spreading over Europe, and still are?"

It's been suggested that Hamilton was guilty of associating Kugelmann's Nazi nature with her German nationality. However, Roach, his alter-ego, makes it quite explicit during this argument: "I'm not talking about nationalities. I'm talking about Nazis."

Nevertheless, one can't escape the feeling that Hamilton is making a point about the essential straightforward goodness of the English. Roach has throughout the book been taunted by Kugelmann as "The English Miss", "Miss Prim", etc. Roach now declares, in so many words, that this is a virtue, that it cuts through the fug of cosmopolitan compromise and dissimulation and gets to the heart of the matter. "I'm just not going to have remarks made like this when people are dying all around us for what they think's right."

Both Bone and Roach are battered and bruised by their Nazi tormentors, and both succeed in vanquishing them at the end. Bone, of course, simply murders Netta and Peter before destroying himself. It's a grim, ironic closure with little light at the end of the tunnel.

Miss Roach on the other hand, although indirectly causing the death of Thwaites, achieves an unlikely but extremely satisfactory triumph. She is able to leave The Rosamund Tea Rooms with her pride intact and fired with a determination to face her fears. It's a more optimistic variation on the climax of *The Plains of Cement*. Ella has the possibility of inheriting money from her sick stepfather, guiltily wishes him dead, but has to endure seeing him miraculously recover. No redemption for poor Ella. Miss Roach, by contrast, inherits almost the same amount of money from a dead relative and is free to enjoy it.

After the pantomime, she finds herself back in London for good. Her boss has booked her into Claridges, it being the only hotel with any rooms to spare. She agonises over which of the two beds in her suite she is going to sleep in (ironically, there is only a double room left for this single lady) and has a bath and settles down to face her, and her country's uncertain future. The final words, as she slips into much deserved sleep, "God help us, God help all of us, every one, all of us", close what has been an exhausting journey.

5

Final Years: The Midnight Bell Tolls

1948-1962 Final novels, the struggle with alcohol, and death.
The Gorse Trilogy, *The West Pier*,
Mr Stimpson and Mr Gorse, Unknown Assailant

After the war, although Hamilton was succeeding professionally, his personal life was becoming more chaotic while his health was increasingly endangered by his addiction to alcohol.

In 1947 he produced a preliminary script for Alfred Hitchcock's film version of his most successful stage play, *Rope*. He worked on the treatment with Sydney Bernstein, with whose Granada company Hitchcock had formed Transatlantic Pictures at Elstree Studios. It proved such an ordeal for Hamilton that he began further sustained heavy drinking. It got so bad that he was forced to enter a nursing home to dry out – the first time this had happened and a sign of worse things to come.

His screenplay was eventually reworked, not once but twice after which Hitchcock himself added parts of the novel during filming! The result, though considered by many movie experts as a classic, depressed him and led to more drinking.

Sometime during 1948-49, he began an extramarital affair with Ursula Stewart, born Lady Ursula Chetwynd-Talbot, an author who published under the name Laura Talbot. For years Hamilton would live with "La", as her friends called her, during the week and return to his wife, Lois, at the weekends. Even after his divorce from Lois in 1953 and his marriage to La in 1954, this triangular love affair continued until his death.

Despite his tumultuous private life, however, Hamilton was able to write three more novels and two radio plays between 1951 and 1955. The novels – the start of an ambitious Comedie Humaine series – concern the sociopath and criminal, Ernest Ralph Gorse.

When the first in the sequence, entitled *The West Pier*, came out in August 1952, the reviews were widespread and favourable. The novelist L.P. Hartley enthused in *The Sunday Times*, "The entertainment value of this brilliantly-told story could hardly be higher." The *Times Literary Supplement* gave it a full page and the BBC, a half-hour talk. Nevertheless, Hamilton felt there was something muted in the praise and that judgement was being suspended – and he began to feel the weight of an expectation he himself had created.

1952 saw another of his radio plays, *Caller Anonymous*, transmitted, a further successful collaboration with Val Gielgud at the BBC. After this he cloistered himself in a house in Whitchurch, Surrey where, nursed by Lois and writing for three hours a day, he produced the second Gorse novel, *Mr Stimpson and Mr Gorse*. Once it was finished, he returned to London in 1953 to nervously await its publication. His fears for the book's public reception had been created by an extraordinary response to the finished manuscript by Michael Sadleir, his publisher and trusted friend. He had not liked the book at all and had criticised it in highly personal terms. As it transpired, the critics and public felt quite differently: it was a huge success.

Soon afterwards, he wrote his final stage play, *The Man Upstairs*, but when it opened in 1954 it was not critically acclaimed and never made it to London's West End. Though now increasingly ill from further bouts of heavy drinking, he made an immense effort in 1955 to finish what would be the third of *The Gorse Trilogy*, and the last of his work to be published, *Unknown Assailant*.

The final years of Hamilton's life were unproductive and difficult. In times of sobriety he worked on two novels, *The Happy Hunting Grounds* and *Memoirs of a Heavy Drinking Man* but neither were completed or published. At one point, he agreed to undergo the Dent cure for alcoholism but, although helped by his brother, the cure failed and he started to drink more than ever. This, combined with his dysfunctional private life, eventually led to severe bouts of depression during which he contemplated committing suicide. On the advice of La's former husband, he underwent electroshock therapy. This caused him to lose his memory for a while but he eventually recovered and, although the depression and suicidal tendencies disappeared, he never wrote anything serious again. Instead, he who had once been uncannily skilful at remodelling the material of his life into works of fiction, now turned inward, satisfying what he called his "wonderful new urge just to scribble" with long letters to his brother and rough, scattered attempts at memoirs. He also started to compile reference books and teach himself Latin and maths.

Fortunately, the receipts of his two plays, *Rope* and *Gaslight*, would continue to provide him with a comfortable income for the rest of his life. Unfortunately, he remained plagued by alcoholism and his health gradually declined due to cirrhosis.

Patrick Hamilton, the Dickens devotee, died aged 58 on 23rd September 1962. Geranium petals from a wreath were scattered on his coffin. Charles Dickens also died in his 58th year, entombed in Westminster Abbey, with his coffin covered with his favourite flower – scarlet geraniums.

The Gorse Trilogy

> *In spite of his worldly astuteness, he may have lived, perhaps, like so many outstanding criminals, a sort of dream-like life. But, even if this were so, the dream was evil.*
>
> Patrick Hamilton

The Gorse Trilogy is ostensibly the study of the inner life of a peculiar type of character from whom, according to the narrator at the start of *The West Pier*, "the most atrocious criminals emerge". The narrator continues, "We feel the poisoner Neil Creame, the bath murderer George Smith and many others of a similar way of thinking belonged to this type." In *Mr Stimpson and Mr Gorse*, the second novel in the trilogy, yet more infamous murderers such as Burke and Hare, Neville Heath and George Haigh are among many others added to the list.

According to Hamilton biographer, Nigel Jones, the notorious double murderer Heath, who was hanged in 1946, influenced Hamilton in a most uncomfortable fashion. "(He) seemed to him to sum up all that was most rotten about England. With his absurd public school and militarist pretensions, his penchant for fast cars and 'popsies', as he called women, he might have stepped out of one of Patrick's own novels."

Jones goes further, suggesting that it was in the darker side of Heath's criminal psyche that Hamilton saw parallels with his own disturbed personality. "Thinking back to his frequent recourse to prostitutes prepared to indulge his own sadistic fantasies, it is little wonder that Patrick the writer saw in Heath the criminal echoes that were worryingly familiar." Thus, *The West Pier* was, "an account of (Neville) Heath's development grafted on to Patrick's early life."

However, the notion is highly contentious, not least because, as the novels progress, Gorse simply bears no resemblance to such a violent sadist such as Heath. On the surface, he's really no more than a minor swindler whose frauds are never even reported to the police.

Curiously, in 2006 the Metropolitan Police revealed a pamphlet they had published in 1947 for the eyes of police forces only, outlining the methods and profiles of scores of conmen and petty swindlers then operating in war-weary England. "Confidence tricksters dress well, frequent the best hotels and restaurants, are popular with the staff (by liberal tipping) are good conversationalists and generally exude an atmosphere of generosity and good feeling ... The visitor finds himself in congenial company with a well-informed and pleasant companion who insists on paying more than his share of the expenses ..."

Among their various tricks was taking bets on races that never happened and persuading victims to invest in bogus stocks and shares. In the second book of the trilogy, Gorse defrauds a Mrs Plumleigh-Bruce thus: he encourages her to gamble on a horse race, so as to reward her with spurious winnings. Since he does not actually place a wager, he is able to ingratiate himself to enable the larger fraud. Did Hamilton, by any chance, have access to this Met document?

The West Pier

For the background to *The West Pier*, Hamilton certainly drew on his Brighton roots while writing the book, for he was living with his wife in Hove Street, very close to the pier itself (then still a thriving pleasure-dome). The critic, Walter Allen, describes *The West Pier* as "a novel of place, and its author was writing about the locations he loved best; his old home in First Avenue, his old school, the county cricket ground, the two piers, the Metropole Hotel, Brighton station. 'Funny,' as Hamilton put it to his brother, 'how one always comes back to Brighton.'"

As the novel starts, we are introduced to Gorse as a schoolboy and shown how he commences his nefarious career in a modest way, hiding a torch to create conflict between fellow pupils, many of whom willingly follow his (anti-Semitic) teasing of Rosen, the wrongly-accused victim. Some time later, the school's headmaster, Mr Codrington, is interviewed by police after a young girl has been robbed near the county cricket ground and tied up in a shed by a fair-haired boy whose green cap she identifies. Codrington half-consciously covers up all possibilities that any of his pupils might have been responsible but later realises that he had failed to tell the policeman that, "as the story had been unfolded the figure of Ernest Ralph Gorse, the boy with the remarkable hair, had flashed at once into his mind". Gorse, although sly and astute, is clearly extremely lucky at crucial moments.

What's more, from the very start, there are those who recognise Gorse's oddly-seductive and yet loathsome qualities. Gorse's widowed stepmother, with whom he lives, finds Gorse's presence more than just unsettling, as the narrative shows:

> Although an extremely fine judge of character, as such a type of ex-barmaid always is, she was unable quite to name to herself what it was which she found so distasteful, if not almost detestable, in her stepson. She contented herself with telling herself (and her intimate friends) that he was a 'funny' one, an 'odd' one, a 'rum' one, and she predicted that his future would be curious. She said that she never knew 'what he was thinking'.

This inscrutability would prove a mixed blessing for both Gorse and his creator.

The central plot-line commences when Gorse and two ex-school chums, Ryan and Bell, are holidaying in Brighton just after the First World War. They pick up two girls, pretty Esther and plain Gertrude, but when Esther and Ryan look like getting together, Gorse – though not interested in Esther sexually – contrives to drive a wedge between them. He does this by writing unpleasant and threatening letters to the two of them, anonymously, of course, made up from words he cuts out from newspaper articles and pastes together.

He then learns that Esther has some money saved up so he devises a swindle involving the buying of a car to defraud her of the cash. His motivation doesn't appear to be primarily financial; instead, it seems to centre upon the empowerment that his deceptions afford him, and the frisson derived from the elaboration of stratagems undertaken to deceive. An implied consequence of his deception is that Esther, a working-class girl from a desperately poor background, will miss out on one of the few big opportunities that life might have offered her for love and advancement. She fritters away her chances by rejecting Ryan and choosing Gorse. Gorse, ruthless to the end, leaves her nothing and appears to enjoy doing it.

At the end, "He had taken her savings: he had recovered her ring; and had deprived her even of the three pounds left over from her savings ... he had most ironically extracted from her what was as good as an admission that she would engage herself to him, or marry him. It is difficult not to believe that, had he desired them, he could have taken from her the clothes in which she stood."

The actor Corin Redgrave, who appeared in a radio episode of the *Trilogy*, describes Hamilton's grasp on villainy. "It's motiveless malignancy. The villain has no other motive than the sheer enjoyment of doing harm."

Gorse's fraudulent methods are meticulous and yet quite simple, combining a convincing persuasiveness with a knowingness about social manners and conformity. He also possesses, as contemporary critic Professor Phil Tew has noted, an uncanny ability to recognise both the innate and extraneous qualities of his victims which he utilises to spitefully manipulate them. He pays great attention to them, thinks carefully and calculatingly about them. Nonetheless, Hamilton emphasises that there was nothing particularly unusual about his skills:

> In much later years it was rumoured that Gorse had Hypnotic Eyes with women. Indeed, pictures of these alleged Hypnotic Eyes, isolated from his face, were published in the newspapers.

> But all this was mere press folly and sensationalism. Gorse had no hypnotic quality: all he did was to use common sense and take the greatest pains in the particular field of activity in which he was naturally gifted.

As Hamilton indicates, "Much as we may dislike the character of Gorse, it must be conceded that he did things thoroughly …" In the process, a curious central truth about con-artistry is revealed – it is very hard, painstaking work, requiring a skill and energy which, if harnessed to do good rather than evil might make the con-man an artist of another sort.

Despite Gorse's obvious unpleasantness, and the fact that he is "endowed with an explicitly satanic degree of indifference to humanity", he is not unlikeable. The monologic narrative voice, compared by one commentator to "a jocular barrister prosecuting a tricky criminal for whom he entertains a sneaky regard", implicates the reader at the expense of the non-Gorse characters. He also seems prone to appalling errors of judgement at times, which underline a certain vulnerability, despite the smooth surface.

Like so much of Hamilton's work, though the implications are bleak, the book makes an extremely amusing read, much of the humour emanating from Ryan and Esther's conversational misunderstandings. Neither of them is confident enough to tell the other about the anonymous postcards Gorse is sending them and which are key to his successful robbing of Esther.

From the moment *The West Pier* was published, however, it would meet with an awkward question posed by various once-supportive critics and influential old friends. Why didn't Hamilton make explicit nor explain Gorse's underlying motives? Graham Greene, it was pointed out, who also created a Brighton-based criminal monster, Pinkie, in *Brighton Rock*, provided a philosophy based on the Catholic religion to underpin events. By stark contrast, the "motiveless nature of (Gorse's) evil hangs enigmatically over all three books."

Phil Tew is in no doubt as to Hamilton's principal achievement, however: "Hamilton's intention was to create a typology, or classification of evil, without retribution, and without offering many clues as to Gorse's inner nature, leaving him as a cold and inwardly inexpressive individual." Thus, "the strength of the books lies in the portrait of a loner with manipulative social skills, edged with sociopathic, psychopathic tendencies, who exists outside of the moral norms and largely beyond the social framework. Hamilton chooses to mirror the potential inscrutability of evildoers. Therein lies both the fascination and power of such perversity."

Nevertheless, back in 1952, Hamilton himself was not so confident, admitting:

> I will never really get into his [Gorse's] skin and have told the reader as much – it is extremely difficult to guess what goes on beneath the surface of their [criminals like Gorse] minds. It is only from their surface behaviour and surface utterances, that the depths can be dimly understood or estimated ...They are, I think, sort of *somnambulists*. They live in a sort of dream – an evil dream ... their criminal behaviour comes and goes in waves – waves which, nearly always, increase in volume and power.

And so his readers waited for something more sinister, for the last line of the novel indicates that Gorse was speeding into London "and to his very curious destination in life."

Mr Stimpson and Mr Gorse

The second novel in the Trilogy, *Mr Stimpson and Mr Gorse*, certainly takes Gorse further, picking up his life almost a decade later. It is also the strongest of the three novels, a major comic achievement and a savage anatomy of English life fired by scorn and even hatred. It would, however, prove to be the straw that broke Hamilton's back as a novelist.

It is set in Reading and opens in the saloon bar of The Friar. Gorse is now 25 years old and when he first arrives on the scene, his principal target, a widow named Mrs Plumleigh-Bruce, already has both a suitor – an estate agent, Mr Stimpson – and a married but lecherous major in attendance. With these two characters, Hamilton covers old ground. The composition of tortuous 'poems' by the major is similar to those of Sounder in *The Midnight Bell* and a brilliant, familiar portrait of drunkenness is presented by the estate agent. Mrs Plumleigh-Bruce, however, is an entirely new creation.

Hamilton makes it hard for the reader to feel much sympathy for her. Biographer Nigel Jones has summed her up perfectly. "She is a plummy-voiced, rabbit-toothed, genteelly foolish dog-owner and oppressor of servants." The intrusive authorial voice once again creates an atmosphere of unpleasantly negative feelings towards her and there are some wickedly effective satirical passages. Hamilton also describes her suburban-kitsch environment with great relish. Of a small room in her house which she used as a study, but which was also intended as a lure for her suitor, Mr Stimpson, the narrator informs us:

> Mrs Plumleigh-Bruce cultivated and, in devious ways, advertised to Mr Stimpson the atmosphere in this room as one suited to the masculine spirit and habit. She alluded to it as a 'Study', as a 'Den', as a 'Snuggery' and as a 'Hidey-Hole'.
>
> Some men, alas, are highly flattered by the notion of being provided with studies, dens, snuggeries or hidey-holes. It makes them feel like they are scholars, smokers, recluses, and clumsy lions.

Gorse quickly decides to swindle her of whatever wealth she possesses and sets about the task by passing himself off as a decorated veteran of the war. His method of persuasion is revealing as is the cold subtlety whereby he reads the vulnerability of his speciality – women. As he explains to Mrs Plumleigh-Bruce:

> In this world one has to do things in the right way – and that means the big way – or not at all, hasn't one? If one does things in the small way – in the Reading way, if I may say so – one never gets anywhere. And, although chance has brought you temporarily to Reading, I know you're not the type of person who does things in the Reading way, the silly, fiddling, petty little middle-class way.

'Doing things the big way' was a line that shamed and flattered his victims at the same time, and was therefore almost irresistible. Inevitably, Gorse succeeds in fleecing and then dumping her. To add to her humiliation, Plumleigh-Bruce's original suitor marries her maid and she herself is forced to retreat, disgraced and considerably poorer, to Worthing.

The ending suggests, enigmatically, that Gorse will eventually die "painlessly and quickly".

When first presented with the manuscript, Hamilton's publisher admitted that he was embarrassed as to what to say about the book:

> Candidly, I am gravely embarrassed what to say about [it] which, despite great technical virtuosity, gives an impression of petulance and of personal prejudices so peevishly overstated as to render the characters mere cockshies. This promises badly for the book's reception by critics and public. I will be thought disagreeable and unsympathetic, because there is not a tolerably likeable person in it. It will strike such reviewers and readers as do not relish your particular and highly individual brand of nonsense (and the notices of *The West Pier* showed that certain recalcitrants do exist) as laboured and facetious. Thirdly, sustained mockery and relentless scarification dealt out by a novelist to characters whom he had purposely presented as grotesque marionettes, bring weariness to a reader and make him long for relief.

Closer to home, Patrick's brother, Bruce, also felt the depiction of Gorse lacked psychological depth, "All that could be done with him, except on a superficial level, was to exhibit, effectively and convincingly, his behaviour. But this sort of job is surely a lesser job, unworthy of a writer of Patrick's gifts, particularly that of carrying understanding of his people, their states of mind, their moods, their deeds and their words, just one step further than most novelists are able to do."

Critic and novelist, Walter Allen, went further, and condemned Hamilton's use of "archetypes", claiming his loyal readership deserved a more naturalistic approach. Hamilton ought, he suggested, to have written a different sort of novel with complex rounded characters, whom readers could respect. Instead, he had, according to Allen, "dodged the novelist's real issue" by going "back to the pre-history of the novel, going back, in fact, to that seventeenth-century literary exercise, the Character."

"They are, as it were, accretions of generalisations about broad categories – real or otherwise – of human beings, given an illusion of life by Mr Hamilton's air of knowingness about their haunts and habit; so much so that they sometimes appear almost as the secretions of their circumstances. Challenge the generalisations and the conviction departs."

Once again, Hamilton was being told off by his closest friends for not writing the novel they would have written! However, his aims had not been recognised and were completely different to theirs. He was using Gorse as an instrument in what was intended to be the first chapter in a savage anatomy of English life. He'd talked of writing a Comedie Humaine, a series of books that aimed to encompass the broad sweep of social types, the vast range of social situations and settings existing in England at that time. It would be an attempt to show man and society in their completeness, as a complex network of interrelations. *Mr Stimpson and Mr Gorse* represented a first step in that direction.

He had written about the lower middle class before, of course: in *Craven House*, and in the *The Slaves of Solitude* and he'd not been kind to some of his principal characters. But those novels had been set either long ago or during a heightened time of conflict. Now he'd stepped firmly into suburbia and, though the book was set in the inter-war years, it could well have been the 1950s, making it a contemporary critique. Having introduced us to Gorse in *The West Pier*, *Mr Stimpson and Mr Gorse* represented the first real step in that direction.

Hamilton had made it clear that he had no interest in extending compassion or understanding to Gorse, nor does he extend it to Gorse's victims. Had the widowed Mrs Plumleigh-Bruce been less vain a woman, she would not have been so easy to flatter and deceive. This stern logic, this relentless misanthropy, did not go down well because Hamilton was no longer dealing exclusively with 'low-life'. Women like Mrs Plumleigh-Bruce were recognisably middle class and 'decent' and so his contempt for his characters could no longer be dismissed as justifiable.

These blackly hilarious portraits are fired by Hamilton's scorn, even hatred, with much cruel fun being made of the pretentiousness and pomposity of suburban lives and taste. It is Moribundia without the science-fiction: what had been allegorical is now realised in savage caricature. His middle class friends didn't like it at all.

For Professor Phil Tew, it's an example of Hamilton, the Marxist, "weaving a political critique, a deeply ironic series of portraits that constitute a phenomenological observation, a cartography of social gullibility, of provincial evil."

For academic John Mepham, however, it was Marxism's *failure* that provided the venom: "After the Second World War Hamilton lost his optimism that a new form of civilisation was possible. He arrived at a bitter and pessimistic vision of modern life. People, he seems to suggest, deserve the awfulness of their suburban and proletarian lives, because they lack the intelligence or courage to do anything about it. His characters are bitterly-drawn portraits of stupidity and wickedness. This shift in his political views may underlie the grimness and pessimism of the *The Gorse Trilogy*."

As Phil Tew has recognised, today this kind of savage, ironic aesthetic, the negative grotesque, the oblique world-view, is familiar to readers of contemporary novelists such as B.S. Johnson, J.G. Ballard, Martin Amis, Jenny Diski, Salman Rushdie, and Jeanette Winterson. No wonder so many of them refer to him with admiration and cite him as an influence.

Michael Sadleir, then in his mid-sixties, can't be blamed for failing to recognise a masterpiece of comedy that struck so forcibly at his own social class. He was clearly judging by a range of aesthetic responses that were fundamentally conservative and traditional and which rendered his position innately antithetical to such a text. Gorse was simply outside Sadleir's comprehension of what constituted creativity.

Despite good reviews from Peter Quennell and John Betjeman, and many others, Hamilton understandably found the attacks wounding. They undermined his self-esteem at a time when his health was failing rapidly. He reacted against the 'misgivings' of the publisher and of friends like J.B. Priestley and his brother by accepting their criticisms. It didn't bode well for the final volume.

Unknown Assailant

Hamilton's final novel is something of an oddity being not much longer than a very long short story. His health was so bad by this time that he had to dictate the book to a secretary and it is, as a result, little more than an outline. Thus, its gestation and physical production have to be taken into account when judging it.

Nevertheless, it is a surprising denouement to the Comedie Humaine, particularly if the loyal reader is expecting Gorse to come to the bad end that Hamilton had regularly been hinting at.

Even worse, gone is the cutting satirical edge and coruscating wit that marks out *Mr Stimpson and Mr Gorse* as a major achievement. By stark contrast to Mrs Plumleigh-Bruce, Gorse's last victim – another gullible naïf, this time called Ivy rather than Esther – hardly seems to suffer at all. In fact, she ultimately appears immune to her financial loss and attempted humiliation, even though Gorse (calling himself the Honourable Gerald Claridge) abandons her in the countryside tied up with a sash-cord.

It is something of a comedown for Gorse, as he has been reduced to simply robbing her because she's forced him (through a combination of luck and pig-headedness) to tell the truth about what he's really up to. Furious though he is, he isn't violent towards her. Quite the reverse. He ties her up using a reef-knot that she can easily slip and as he leaves her, says, "Well – goodbye. And you're sure you can get free?" To which she replies, "Yes. Goodbye. And thank you very much indeed." Hardly Neville Heath, who was known to drink the blood of his victims!

The only loser is her vain, preening father, the odious Mr Barton, yet another thinly disguised portrait of Hamilton senior painted in vicious strokes of loathing. Gorse inveigles him into investing in a musical play, entitled *You and Me* but pockets the money before it reaches the play's producers. *You and Me* is a roaring success, but Barton, despite advice from others which might have alerted him to the fraud, benefits not at all – in fact, he's lost £200. Even then, Hamilton makes it clear that he might still have recouped his loss if his own unpleasant nature hadn't got in the way.

As Ivy builds herself a new life in a village community that welcomes her after her ordeal, we realise we are witnessing something of a happy ending. She loses her savings but she was "curiously disinterested in money" and had only saved because she'd been told to. She also didn't care for her father and he didn't care for her so the fact that she never returns home suits both parties.

As for the much-celebrated 'tying-up scene', this is necessary simply in order that Gorse can escape. It is not suggested that Gorse is deriving any sort of sordid pleasure from it. Hamilton himself has already attempted to defuse the sinister overtones of such practices earlier in the book by explaining:

> Gorse, though normally rather sexless, had bouts of great physical passion, and when these came upon him he was mostly stimulated by what is (on the whole foolishly) known as perversion. He liked to tie women up in order to get the impression that they were at his mercy, and he also liked to be tied up by women and to feel that he was at theirs. It is foolish to call this perversion because, as every serious student of the general psychology of sex (who would be supported by any prostitute, or keeper or frequenter of brothels) knows, it is merely a rather emphasised form of the sadistic or masochistic element underlying every physical relationship between man and woman, or, if it comes to that, man and man, or woman and woman.

That is to say, we all do it in one form or another. Hamilton's idea may have been that all relations between men and women include an element of sexual sadism, but he was never able to openly explore this in his novels.

And so his last major work ends, not with a bang but a whimper, and with Gorse ensconced, not on Death Row, but "on the outskirts of Birmingham, in a small boarding house, in which he was looked upon as a decided dog and a wag".

If we compare these three novels with the ones that make up *Twenty Thousand Streets Under The Sky*, we can see clearly the decline in Hamilton's powers as a writer. What's missing from the three Gorse books is any cumulative weight of emotion and narrative depth as the stories unfold. In *Twenty Thousand Streets Under the Sky*, by the time we reach the third novel, the narrative has become heart-breaking, genuinely moving and emotionally engaging. There is innocence and lightness at the beginning, but heartbreak at the end.

Where Gorse is concerned, although the level of intensity rises powerfully during the second novel, Hamilton appears to have no energy left to find another level, and the series peters out into chatty, almost cheeky inconsequence. Whether Hamilton would have returned to Gorse if his health had not deteriorated is not known. As it was, his health was so bad, he could no longer contemplate any sustained work.

Yet it would be wrong to accept J.B. Priestley's verdict, that "Hamilton no longer had the creative energy to bamboozle us into believing it was a good idea". *The Gorse Trilogy* remains an intriguing and, at times, mesmerising work, establishing a peculiar individual who really ought, by now, to be established as one of English literature's immortal 'characters'.

6

Hamilton on Stage and Screen

*Films are fundamentally no good because they are ephemeral.
You must either write printed books or printed plays.*
                                                    Patrick Hamilton

Patrick Hamilton professed to disapprove of the whole cinematic genre and considering the generally poor quality of the films based on his work, he had a point. At least two of these movies are considered to have been successful, however, one of which is now considered a classic.

In 1929 he'd written the stage play *Rope* (entitled *Rope's End* in America), which proved a critical and commercial success on both sides of the Atlantic. It established Hamilton's reputation as a master of theatrical suspense and continues to appear on major stages today.

How far the play reflected Hamilton's personal interest in Nietzsche's philosophy is, as with his 'conversion' to Marxism, a matter of debate. There is no doubt that Hamilton was greatly interested in Nietzsche's work, in particular, *Thus Spake Zarathustra*. He was attracted by its simplified idea of the 'Superman': the gifted exception to the common run of humanity, destined by force of will to stamp his mark on the world. He wrote of his own capacities: "I know the difference between failure or half-failure and success in this life is the difference between mild-self-control and something partially fanatical." The title of the play, in fact, derives from a Nietzsche aphorism: "Man is a rope, fastened between animal and Superman – a rope over an abyss."

Such delving beneath its surface, however, always irritated Hamilton. "It's thriller, a thriller of all time, and nothing but a thriller," he insisted.

In 1948, Alfred Hitchcock, long an admirer of Hamilton's work, produced and directed a screen adaptation of the play as his first independent production. Hitchcock engaged Hamilton as a screenwriter: $3,000 for the rights and $300 a week for the scripting. Filming began in January 1948 and *Rope* was released the following year in Britain.

Hamilton later professed to enjoy the work: "Doing *Rope* was exciting as well as exhausting. In colour, if you please! – and all indoors with five rooms – a Hitchcock stunt. The camera, like an invisible man, simply walks about the flat … And sees and hears everything. Never done before, and so, as you can imagine, a difficult job for an inexperienced screenwriter."

Rope would become something of a cinematic classic as an experiment in suspense. Vincent Canby of the *New York Times* explains, "Hitchcock was interested in seeing whether he could find a cinematic equivalent to the play, which takes place in the actual length of time of the story. To do this, he decided to shoot it in what would appear to be one long, continuous 'take', without cutaways or any other breaks in the action. In fact there would have to be a disguised break every 10 minutes, which was as much film as the camera could contain. These breaks he usually accomplishes by having the camera appear to pan across someone's back, during which dark close-ups the film reel was changed. Not all of these disguises are equally effective as Hitchcock himself later realised. However, his obsession with telling a story without resorting to the usual methods of montage, and without cutting from one shot to another, resulted in a film of unusual, fascinating technical facility."

However, it wasn't a satisfying experience for Hamilton. Losing control over one's work is always a traumatic business for an author, especially one as private as Hamilton. His collaboration with a British producer, Sydney Bernstein, at Elstree Studios was scrapped and the version he eventually produced went into several rewrites. He played no part in these and, although he was told he would be able to go to Hollywood to work on the final version, Hitchcock ultimately overlooked him.

Hitchcock, as ever, was the dominant influence throughout, gradually moving the script away from Hamilton's original and towards his own conception of it. As the film went into production

Hitchcock subtly introduced into the project a vein of perverse humour as well as emphasising what he felt was the implicit homosexuality of the piece. As the movie opens, Brandon, who dominates his homosexual lover, Philip, is in the process of strangling the unfortunate David with a piece of ordinary clothesline – something that did not occur in Hamilton's original. The strangling soon becomes a source of savagely unfunny jokes: referring to the rigours of murderer Brandon's piano practice, unknowing characters casually utter ironic phrases like "Knock 'em dead!" and "These hands will bring you fame!" and, "I could strangle you!"

The final impression left by the film, according to Hitchcock's biographer Donald Spoto, is "not one of admiration for a difficult technique ... This first film under Hitchcock's control as a producer is in fact his coldest work: its obsessive methodology never conceals its misanthropy."

Rope still has a special place in most Hitchcock fans' perceptions of his work. It was, however, quite a shock to Hamilton, who considered it "sordid and practically meaningless balls".

It has been suggested that he found Hitchcock's version unsatisfactory because, while his own public face was that of a charming but private man, here on a vast screen he saw ideas from which he had distanced himself 20 years earlier, blown up and made darkly hilarious. As biographer Sean French suggests, Hamilton's objections to the film were not because Hitchcock had *betrayed* his play but that he explored its implications all too painfully, expertly teasing out what had given the play its perverse effectiveness in the first place.

On release, several social and educational associations across America condemned the film as undesirable and dangerous.

After *Rope*, Hamilton concentrated on writing novels, interspersed with the occasional radio play and didn't return to writing for the stage until 1938, when he produced another hit, *Gaslight* (also called *Angel Street* and *5 Chelsea Lane*).

Hamilton claimed he wrote *Gaslight* (which he subtitled "a Victorian thriller") as a pastiche, employing dialogue that was far more conventional than that in his novels. Nevertheless, it continues to fascinate and enjoys periodic 'resurrections.'

It opened in the West End of London in 1939 and then in New

York, where it had the longest run of a foreign play in Broadway history. By 1944 it had already been filmed twice, most famously in the George Cukor version, starring Ingrid Bergman and Charles Boyer. In 2007 it opened again at London's Old Vic theatre, and caused quite a stir.

Gaslight is a play in which an arch-villain called Mr Manningham, obsessed with finding the jewels belonging to an old woman he once murdered, drives his wife to the brink of insanity before salvation materialises in the kindly form of a retired detective called Rough. Not the stuff of great dramatic literature, but Hamilton possessed the knack of pulling out every stop to keep audiences glued to the edge of their seats. His "stroke of genius", as one of Hamilton's biographers, Nigel Jones, observed, was an idea that he drew from a story by his elder brother Bruce. In 1938, he remembered a detail from Bruce's first novel, *To Be Hanged*, which had been published eight years earlier. The hero is questioning a landlady about one of her lodgers:

> She thought she was mighty smart, slipping away quietly when I was washing up in the scullery. But I always knew when she'd gone, because the gas in the kitchen went up brighter when she turned it out in the sitting-room. And she didn't go up to bed, neither, unless she undressed in the dark, because it would have gone down again when she turned the light on upstairs ...

Hamilton spotted that this idea would work much more powerfully on stage, where the audience could actually witness it. Thus, Manningham's secret nightly trips to the attic to search for the hidden treasure, involve a dipping of the gaslight in the rest of the house – adding to Mrs Manningham's psychological torment and the satisfying murk of malignancy. Not only did he borrow it for his new play, but it also supplied him with the title, *Gaslight*.

Even though melodramas were already considered passé in 1938 when *Angel Street* premiered, its multitude of suspense elements proved there was life in the well-made Victorian spine-tingler after all. As Elyse Sommer, reviewing a 1999 New York production enthused, "a diabolical killer and seducer, spousal abuse in the parlour and probably the bedroom as well, bigamy, lost rubies, mysterious footfalls and light shifts, locked drawers and rooms and an insistently persistent policeman – that's a fairly complete list of the elements Hamilton managed to cram into his three acts!"

Hamilton also shows himself able to understand both the plight of the abused wife, and the detached sociopathic game of the husband. One of the dark successes of the piece is its play with the idea of madness – the weird rationale and logic of the psychopath, the confusion of his victim – a territory he would revisit in some detail for *The Gorse Trilogy*.

The most recent of the play's directors enthused in June 2007:

> It's difficult to talk about it, because it doesn't pretend to be anything other than a thriller in the Victorian manner, but it's a thriller written by someone who can really write. He pitches you into the situation between the husband and wife within three lines of the opening. You don't know how you get into the terror – it just happens after about three sentences.

In fact, the play begins with a scene in which the manipulative, sly husband is undermining the wife, tormenting her, alternately buoying her up and being kind, then swiftly dashing her down and accusing her of things (we know) she hasn't done. She's fragile and clearly under his thumb and he's particularly cruel. She is then visited by a retired policeman who, apart from reassuring her as to her sanity and coming across as a reliable and kind man, reveals the secret of her house and the behaviour of her husband.

Far from being passé, the play, was, according to director, Peter Gill, ahead of its time. "Without wishing to sound too portentous about it, you can see the hint of a play that, in a different world, in a different theatre, he might have written – about sex."

The flirtatious relationship that Manningham has with his maid-servant (one of the many means by which he sadistically undermines his wife) is telling: "The maid is very important in creating the atmosphere of the play, suggesting the kind of middle-class marriage where the wife is neurotic and not available to her husband. *Gaslight* is not a feminist play but it's a marvellous portrait of a desolate marriage. It's hetero-hell."

The actress Rosamund Pike playing the wife, Bella Manningham, agreed:

> The sexual tension is partly what breaks the play from its faintly ironic bondage of 'a Victorian thriller'. A master is obsessed with a maid, and a maid is obsessed with claiming sexual victory over her mistress. It is a good play because it is fuelled by obsession: a woman who obsesses over her sanity, a husband obsessed with re-enacting something in a house he once knew 20 years ago, and a detective obsessed with solving a crime.

Pike felt that what confirmed Hamilton as a great writer was his understanding of the insidiousness in outwardly mundane situations. "His play explores the treachery of middle-class values, the enforced 'quietening' of the middle-class wife." The maid, Nancy, with all the patter of the street and the pub – a world Hamilton loved – is able to express herself without censure. She deplores Bella's cautious 'how to be kind to the servants' manner, preferring the straight-talking of her husband:

> Bella is trapped in the middle-class niceties of tea and muffins – comforting on one level, but woefully evasive on another. She escapes into make-believe, and even when a rescuer arrives in the form of Detective Rough, it takes the whisky bottle to rescue her from the sham of 'Nothing's wrong' and 'Would you like some sugar?' Bella has been in thrall to her husband, and it takes an equally but differently powerful figure to release her. Any anger she might have felt has been turned against herself; all its energy has been knotted into worry and self-doubt and blame, a horribly accurate and detailed portrait of domestic abuse.

The play also demonstrates Hamilton's understanding of the seductive powers of alcohol, the "medicine from Scotland" administered by Detective Rough, that has the power of removing Bella Manningham's fears and doubt.

The first film version, variously titled *Gaslight* and *Angel Street*, was made in 1940 by British National studios and starred Anton Walbrook and Diana Wynyard. The film was one of the most highly regarded thrillers ever made in England and was a huge success with audiences in Britain and elsewhere. When American film company MGM decided to do a remake, starring international stars Ingrid

Bergman and Charles Boyer, the studio was so concerned about the quality of the earlier British production that it suppressed the original version with the intention of obliterating it, at one point ordering the destruction of all known prints (an instruction that wasn't carried out). Nevertheless, MGM's version, directed by George Cukor, became a Hollywood classic and earned Bergman an Oscar for Best Actress.

Adaptations of Hamilton's novels, whether on stage, film or later television, fared less well. In 1945, Twentieth Century-Fox produced *Hangover Square* but chose to set it, not in pre-War London's seedy Earls Court but in the Edwardian period in opulent West End houses. They transformed George Harvey Bone into a crazed composer (and strangler) played by Laird Cregar who stalked women in London. A schizophrenic genius, he gets a warning pain in the neck whenever he is about to go into one of his blank, murderous spells which take him away from his piano and out into the murky night in search of victims. His transformation from man to beast is accomplished with wild grimaces and clutchings at his neck in a manner reminiscent of Frankenstein's monster.

The *New York Times* reviewer on 8th February 1945 wrote: "When he is not absorbed in composing a concerto, Laird Cregar is a hard-working homicidal maniac. Twentieth Century-Fox burned up a plushy replica of a rich, turn-of-the-century English home to give the film a 'hot' ending. It might be observed, too, that the studio also gleefully put the torch to everything except the title of the Hamilton novel in making this picture, for any resemblance between screen version and the original would be more than 'accidental' – it would be miraculous."

In a macabre twist to reality, Cregar, who had urged the novel on the studio, died as an indirect result of the crash diet he endured to slim down for the role.

Since *Gaslight*, apart from a feeble British attempt to film *The Siege of Pleasure* in 1963, the film industry has left Hamilton's work alone. Intriguingly, it is television that is increasingly looking to re-present his work to a new public.

In 1987, nearly 40 years after it was written, *Mr Stimpson and Mr Gorse* was adapted into the series *The Charmer*, starring Nigel Havers. There was, unfortunately, little attempt on behalf of its makers to retain crucial elements of the book. What's more, as Phil Tew has recognised, Gorse was given both a social *and* a sexual desire as key motivating impulses, the result being that his original, lonely malevolence is considerably diminished. In the book, Gorse seems incapable of such an extended or complex emotion as desire; in *The Charmer*, by contrast, his sexual needs and transgressions are explicitly intertwined. There are also crucial distortions to the original plot. Not only does he impregnate and marry the daughter of a car dealer, a character not in Hamilton's text, he then accidentally kills her in an insurance fraud fire. He then murders an RAF officer in order to steal his identity and uniform. Hamilton's Gorse, of course, hardly lays a finger on anyone.

However, the creative tide would appear to be changing. To mark the centenary of his birth in 2004, BBC4 recently adapted *Twenty Thousand Streets Under the Sky* for the small screen. Writer Kevin Elyot, director Simon Curtis and producer Kate Harwood exercised great care, patience and good taste to produce the three dramas that were not only moving and distinctive, but allowed a new generation to discover, in part at least, the virtues and the concerns of this much neglected British author.

Postscript: Be Always Drunken

If you would not feel the horrible burden of Time weighing on your shoulders and crushing you to the earth, be drunken continually.

Charles Baudelaire

That Hamilton was an alcoholic and died of the consequences will always be a major part of his story. That he wrote so compellingly about the effects of alcohol and was, to quote biographer Sean French, "a connoisseur of alcoholic behaviour" only serves to keep the topic to the fore in any consideration of his life and achievements.

In the late 1970s, an American psychiatrist called Donald Goodwin conducted a study of the big names in 20th-century American literature, and found that 71 percent of them "drank to excess – a rate far higher than any other profession surveyed". His theory was that there is some crucial point in the human makeup where writing, schizophrenia and alcoholism meet. He summed it up thus: "Creative writing requires a rich fantasy life; loners have rich fantasy lives – the ultimate loner is the schizophrenic who lives in a prison of fantasy. Alcohol promotes fantasy." Therefore alcohol helps writing, being alone and having a multiple personality.

In 1987 an American professor carried out a 15-year study of 30 creative writers on the faculty of the Iowa Writers' Workshop where students and faculty have included well-known writers such as Philip Roth, Kurt Vonnegut, John Irving, John Cheever, Robert Lowell and Flannery O'Connor. She was searching for a correlation between schizophrenia and creativity, but she found none.

She did discover, however, that 30 percent of the writers were alcoholics, compared with seven percent in the comparison group of non-writers. She also found that 80 percent of the writers had had an episode of affective disorders, i.e. a major bout of depression including manic-depressive illness, compared with 30 percent in the control group. Two thirds of the ill writers had received psychiatric treatment for their disorders. Two of the 30 committed suicide during the 15 years of the study. She had no decisive explanation to offer as to why this was so.

Hamilton once commented in an interview that writing was a tough business, something that required infinitely more labour and pain than what the average person thought of as work. Indeed, compared to ordinary work, where people were in contact with others, conversed, met new people, were stimulated by human contact, "working at writing seems to me in comparison like hard labour in solitary – something to which even illness is preferable."

Contemporary writer A.L. Kennedy's most recent book, *Paradise*, is a fictional portrait of an alcoholic on the downward arc of her habit. Kennedy herself doesn't drink, she says, because it "just doesn't agree with me", but adds, "this is not a great lifestyle. It's isolated and isolating. You work alone, which is very quiet and intense." A writer will do anything, she explains, to "damp down the emotions, distract them from their own brains."

Towards the end of his life, Hamilton turned to the question of his own addiction: *Memoirs of a Heavy Drinking Man* was intended to examine this. It would be, he wrote, "A personal history, whose main theme is an illness. The illness, in its mildest form, may be called heavy drinking: in its acutest form it may be called imperatively necessary drinking. Like sustenance to a starving man, or insulin to a diabetic, drink is necessary to the victim." He never finished the book, but during this period he did answer two students who were curious as to the genesis of his 'alcoholism'.

The first question was whether his condition could have been genetic. He pointed out that both his father and sister were alcoholics and his brother drank heavily. He also felt the deep insecurities of his childhood and the "agony" of his adolescence contributed along with the overbearing influence his mother had on him. Her eventual suicide also affected him deeply.

Freudian psychology has held that creativity is a sublimation of aggressive and sexual impulses or a response to emotional pain. A domineering, cold mother or any kind of unhappy childhood, according to this view, causes neurosis and anxiety, and neurosis is a veritable hotbed, or incubator, for creativity. Proponents of this theory point out that those same anxieties could cause alcoholism in writers and other artists.

Secondly, Hamilton admitted that he had also been emotionally and sexually frustrated all his life and suffered from an inability to achieve sexual consummation. This, too, encouraged his drinking. Even when he did achieve sexual fulfilment, it caused yet more problems.

Finally, he mentioned that his car accident had damaged him professionally and personally at a pivotal moment in his life. This, too, had driven him to drinking.

Pathography is a style of biography that overemphasises the negative aspects, the sensational underside, of a person's life such as failure, unhappiness, illness and tragedy. Sean French wryly observed that his subject could "describe his own pathography with the precision of a clinician."

But perhaps the search for a mysterious 'connection' between writing success and drink is to look at things much too simplistically. A 1987 article in *The American Scholar* by Julie M. Irwin entitled 'F. Scott Fitzgerald's Little Drinking Problem' took a new look at Fitzgerald's drinking and tried to assess how it affected his writing.

Between 1933 and 1937, Fitzgerald was hospitalized eight times for alcoholism and arrested at least as often. He abused gossip columnist Sheilah Graham, who lived with him. Irwin writes, "We know that alcoholism made Fitzgerald's days hellish and clearly brought about his early demise. Yet given that Fitzgerald worked with this considerable handicap, his productivity becomes all the more impressive ... Knowing that Fitzgerald worked under the pressure of alcoholism makes him seem not like an elegant wastrel ... but a literary craftsman devoted to producing art regardless of the obstacles that stood in his way. This, finally, is the lesson to be learned from Fitzgerald's alcoholism: He was a writer who was also the victim of a disease, not a self-destructive drunk bent on wasting the talent he was given."

This could be seen to be exactly the case with Hamilton, the case as he clearly understood it himself. His continual fight to control his addiction attests to this as he strove hard all his life to produce the novels that are his epitaph. He painfully endured 'dry' days and weeks when he followed a strict, almost monastic regime in order to literally grind the words out. His last novel was produced almost through gritted teeth, so badly was he suffering. The miracle is that, despite his affliction, he had the willpower to go on and surmount the obstacles in his way.

References and Further Reading

Biographies
Patrick Hamilton: A Life, Sean French (Faber & Faber, London, 1993).
The Light Went Out: The Life of Patrick Hamilton, by his brother, Bruce Hamilton, (Constable, London, 1972).
Through a Glass Darkly: The Life of Patrick Hamilton, Nigel Jones (Scribners, London, 1992).

Articles
Patrick Hamilton Interview, Boston Evening Transcript, 21 June 1930.
'Love and death in London's publand' John Branston (*Morning Star*, 3rd November 2004).
'Patrick Hamilton Biography, Bruce Eder (*All Media Guide*, LLC 1168 Oak Valley Drive, Ann Arbor, MI 48108).
'Patrick Hamilton and the Sound of Politics' by Geoff Gilbert (*Core International Journal of the Humanities* 1.2, Fall 2001).
'Fitzrovian Nights', Simon W. Goulding (*Literary London Conference and Journal*, Department of English, Liverpool Hope University College, Hope Park, Liverpool, L16 9JD).
Impromptu in Moribundia by Patrick Hamilton: A far cry from *Hangover Square*, Francis King (*The Spectator*, 6th May 2000).
'War, Conversation, and Context in Patrick Hamilton's *The Slaves of Solitude*', Thierry Labica (*Connotations* 12.1, 2002/2003, pp.72-82) Eberhard-Karls-Universitat Tubingen, Department of English, Wilhelmstr. 50, 72074 Tubingen, Germany.
'Satirising the bourgeois worldview: Patrick Hamilton's *Impromptu in Moribundia*' by Neil Maycroft (*Capital & Class*, 22nd December 2004).
'Patrick Hamilton', John Mepham, Kingston University. (*The Literary Encyclopaedia*, 12th November 2001, The Literary Dictionary Company).
'Getting Dark Now: Patrick Hamilton, *The Slaves of Solitude* and *Hangover*

Square, Leo Mellor (Buzzwords http://www.buzzwords.ndo.co.uk.html).

'World upon World, Genre and History: Patrick Hamilton's *Impromptu in Moribundia*, by Brian McKenna (Journal article; *Utopian Studies*, Vol. 10, no. 1, pp. 69-85.1999).

'Confessions of a heavy-drinking Marxist: Addiction in the work of Patrick Hamilton' by Brian McKenna, *Beyond the Pleasure Dome: Writing and Addiction from the Romantics*, S. Vice, T. Campbell & T. Armstrong eds. (Sheffield Academic Press, 1994).

'Unhappy hour', Dan Rhodes (*The Guardian*, Saturday, 13 March 2004).

'Pulped fictions', Iain Sinclair (*The Guardian* Saturday, 12 March 2005).

'Patrick Hamilton', John Russell Taylor (*London Magazine* Vol. 6, No. 4, May 1966, 58)

'A Phenomenology of the Suffering of Others: the Case of Ralph Ernest Gorse', Prof. Philip Tew (*Critical Engagements,* UK Network for Modern Fiction Studies, Spring/Summer 2007, Vol.1, No.1).

'Whisky Sour', Laura Thompson (*The Independent on Sunday*, 14 March 2004).

'Writers and Alcohol', Ann Waldron (Special to *The Washington Post*, 14 March 1989).

'The saloon bar society: Patrick Hamilton's fiction in the 1930s', P.J. Widdowson, *The 1930s: A Challenge to Orthodoxy*, ed. J. Lucas (Harvester Press, Sussex, 1978).

'English Fiction in the 1930s', Peter J. Widdowson (*Culture and Crisis in Britain in the 1930s*, (London, Lawrence and Wishart, 1979), pp.117-137.

Hamilton Editions

Impromptu in Moribundia (Trent Editions, 1999)
Twenty Thousand Streets Under the Sky (Vintage, 1999)
The Slaves of Solitude (Constable, 1972)
Gaslight : A Victorian Thriller in Three Acts (Constable & Robinson, 1975)
Hangover Square: A Story of Darkest Earl's Court (Penguin Books, 2001)
Craven House (Constable, 1926)
The Gorse Trilogy (Penguin Books, 1992)

Publication dates of Patrick Hamilton's works

(All published by Constable)
Monday Morning 1925
Craven House 1926
Tuppence Coloured 1928

Rope (play) 1929
The Procuration of Judea (play) 1930
John Brown's Body (play) 1930
The Midnight Bell 1929
The Siege of Pleasure 1932
The Plains of Cement 1934
Twenty Thousand Streets Under the Sky 1935
Gaslight (play) 1939
Money with Menaces and *To The Public Danger* (radio plays) 1939
Impromptu in Moribundia 1939
Hangover Square 1941
This is Impossible (pub. French) 1942
The Duke in Darkness (play) 1943
The Slaves of Solitude 1947
Caller Anonymous (radio play) 1952
The West Pier 1951
Mr Stimpson and Mr Gorse 1953
The Man Upstairs (radio play) 1954
Unknown Assailant 1955

GREENWICH EXCHANGE BOOKS

STUDENT GUIDE LITERARY SERIES

The Greenwich Exchange Student Guide Literary Series is a collection of critical essays of major or contemporary serious writers in English and selected European languages. The series is for the student, the teacher and 'common readers' and is an ideal resource for libraries. The *Times Educational Supplement* praised these books, saying, "The style of [this series] has a pressure of meaning behind it. Readers should learn from that ... If art is about selection, perception and taste, then this is it."

(ISBN prefix 978-1-871551 applies unless marked* when 978-1-906075 applies).
All books are paperbacks unless otherwise stated.

The series includes:
Antonin Artaud by Lee Jamieson (98-3)
W.H. Auden by Stephen Wade (36-5)
Honoré de Balzac by Wendy Mercer (48-8)
William Blake by Peter Davies (27-3)
The Brontës by Peter Davies (24-2)
Robert Browning by John Lucas (59-4)
Lord Byron by Andrew Keanie (83-9)
Samuel Taylor Coleridge by Andrew Keanie (64-8)
Joseph Conrad by Martin Seymour-Smith (18-1)
William Cowper by Michael Thorn (25-9)
Charles Dickens by Robert Giddings (26-9)
Emily Dickinson by Marnie Pomeroy (68-6)
John Donne by Sean Haldane (23-5)
Ford Madox Ford by Anthony Fowles (63-1)
The Stagecraft of Brian Friel by David Grant (74-7)
Robert Frost by Warren Hope (70-9)
Patrick Hamilton by John Harding (99-0)
Thomas Hardy by Sean Haldane (33-4)
Seamus Heaney by Warren Hope (37-2)
Joseph Heller by Anthony Fowles (84-6)
Gerard Manley Hopkins by Sean Sheehan (77-3)
James Joyce by Michael Murphy (73-0)
Philip Larkin by Warren Hope (35-8)
Laughter in the Dark – The Plays of Joe Orton by Arthur Burke (56-3)

George Orwell by Warren Hope (42-6)
Sylvia Plath by Marnie Pomeroy (88-4)
Poets of the First World War by John Greening (79-2)
Philip Roth by Paul McDonald (72-3)
Shakespeare's *King Lear* by Peter Davies (95-2)
Shakespeare's *Macbeth* by Matt Simpson (69-3)
Shakespeare's *The Merchant of Venice* by Alan Ablewhite (96-9)
Shakespeare's *A Midsummer Night's Dream* by Matt Simpson (90-7)
Shakespeare's *Much Ado About Nothing* by Matt Simpson (01-9)*
Shakespeare's Non-Dramatic Poetry by Martin Seymour-Smith (22-6)
Shakespeare's *Othello* by Matt Simpson (71-6)
Shakespeare's Second Tetralogy: *Richard II – Henry V* by John Lucas (97-6)
Shakespeare's Sonnets by Martin Seymour-Smith (38-9)
Shakespeare's *The Tempest* by Matt Simpson (75-4)
Shakespeare's *Twelfth Night* by Matt Simpson (86-0)
Shakespeare's *The Winter's Tale* by John Lucas (80-3)
Tobias Smollett by Robert Giddings (21-1)
Alfred, Lord Tennyson by Michael Thorn (20-4)
Dylan Thomas by Peter Davies (78-5)
William Wordsworth by Andrew Keanie (57-0)
W.B. Yeats by John Greening (34-1)

LITERATURE & BIOGRAPHY

Matthew Arnold and 'Thyrsis' *by Patrick Carill Connolly*
Matthew Arnold (1822-1888) was a leading poet, intellect and aesthete of the Victorian epoch. He is now best known for his strictures as a literary and cultural critic, and educationist. After a long period of neglect, his views have come in for a re-evaluation. Arnold's poetry remains less well known, yet his poems and his understanding of poetry, which defied the conventions of his time, were central to his achievement.

The author traces Arnold's intellectual and poetic development, showing how his poetry gathers its meanings from a lifetime's study of European literature and philosophy. Connolly's unique exegesis of 'Thyrsis' draws upon a wide-ranging analysis of the pastoral and its associated myths in both classical and native cultures. This study shows lucidly and in detail how Arnold encouraged the intense reflection of the mind on the subject placed before it, believing in " … the all importance of the choice of the subject, the necessity of accurate observation; and subordinate character of expression."

Patrick Carill Connolly gained his English degree at Reading University

and taught English literature abroad for a number of years before returning to Britain. He is now a civil servant living in London.
2004 • 180 pages • ISBN 978-1-871551-61-7

The Author, the Book and the Reader *by Robert Giddings*
This collection of essays analyses the effects of changing technology and the attendant commercial pressures on literary styles and subject matter. Authors covered include Charles Dickens, Tobias Smollett, Mark Twain, Dr Johnson and John le Carré.
1991 • 220 pages • illustrated • ISBN 978-1-871551-01-3

Norman Cameron *by Warren Hope*
Cameron's poetry was admired by Auden; celebrated by Dylan Thomas; valued by Robert Graves. He was described by Martin Seymour-Smith as "one of ... the most rewarding and pure poets of his generation ..." and is at last given a full-length biography. This eminently sociable man, who had periods of darkness and despair, wrote little poetry by comparison with others of his time, but always of a consistently high quality – imaginative and profound.
Warren Hope is a poet, a critic and university lecturer. He lives and works in Philadelphia, where he raised his family.
2000 • 226 pages • ISBN 978-1-871551-05-1

Aleister Crowley and the Cult of Pan *by Paul Newman*
Few more nightmarish figures stalk English literature than Aleister Crowley (1875-1947), poet, magician, mountaineer and agent provocateur. In this groundbreaking study, Paul Newman dives into the occult mire of Crowley's works and fishes out gems and grotesqueries that are by turns ethereal, sublime, pornographic and horrifying. Like Oscar Wilde before him, Crowley stood in "symbolic relationship to his age" and to contemporaries like Rupert Brooke, G.K. Chesterton and the Portuguese modernist, Fernando Pessoa. An influential exponent of the cult of the Great God Pan, his essentially 'pagan' outlook was shared by major European writers as well as English novelists like E.M. Forster, D.H. Lawrence and Arthur Machen.
Paul Newman lives in Cornwall. Editor of the literary magazine *Abraxas*, he has written over ten books.
2004 • 222 pages • ISBN 978-1-871551-66-2

John Dryden *by Anthony Fowles*
Of all the poets of the Augustan age, John Dryden was the most worldly. Anthony Fowles traces Dryden's evolution from 'wordsmith' to major poet. This critical study shows a poet of vigour and technical panache whose art

was forged in the heat and battle of a turbulent polemical and pamphleteering age. Although Dryden's status as a literary critic has long been established, Fowles draws attention to his neglected achievements as a translator of poetry. He deals also with the less well-known aspects of Dryden's work – his plays and occasional pieces.

Born in London and educated at the Universities of Oxford and Southern California, Anthony Fowles began his career in film-making before becoming an author of film and television scripts and more than twenty books. Readers will welcome the many contemporary references to novels and film with which Fowles illuminates the life and work of this decisively influential English poetic voice.

2003 • 292 pages • ISBN 978-1-871551-58-7

The Good That We Do *by John Lucas*
John Lucas' book blends fiction, biography and social history in order to tell the story of his grandfather, Horace Kelly. Headteacher of a succession of elementary schools in impoverished areas of London, 'Hod' Kelly was also a keen cricketer, a devotee of the music hall, and included among his friends the great trade union leader Ernest Bevin. In telling the story of his life, Lucas has provided a fascinating range of insights into the lives of ordinary Londoners from the First World War until the outbreak of the Second World War. Threaded throughout is an account of such people's hunger for education, and of the different ways government, church and educational officialdom ministered to that hunger. *The Good That We Do* is both a study of one man and of a period when England changed, drastically and forever.

John Lucas is Professor Emeritus of the Universities of Loughborough and Nottingham Trent. He is the author of numerous works of a critical and scholarly nature and has published eight collections of poetry.

2001 • 214 pages • ISBN 978-1-871551-54-9

D.H. Lawrence: The Nomadic Years, 1919-1930 *by Philip Callow*
This book provides a fresh insight into Lawrence's art as well as his life. Candid about the relationship between Lawrence and his wife, it shows nevertheless the strength of the bond between them. If no other book persuaded the reader of Lawrence's greatness, this does.

Philip Callow was born in Birmingham and studied engineering and teaching before he turned to writing. He has published 14 novels, several collections of short stories and poems, a volume of autobiography, and biographies on the lives of Chekhov, Cezanne, Robert Louis Stevenson, Walt Whitman and Van Gogh all of which have received critical acclaim. His biography of D.H. Lawrence's early years, *Son and Lover*, was widely praised.

2006 • 226 pages • ISBN 978-1-871551-82-2

Liar! Liar!: Jack Kerouac – Novelist *by R.J. Ellis*
The fullest study of Jack Kerouac's fiction to date. It is the first book to devote an individual chapter to every one of his novels. *On the Road*, *Visions of Cody* and *The Subterraneans* are reread in-depth, in a new and exciting way. *Visions of Gerard* and *Doctor Sax* are also strikingly reinterpreted, as are other daringly innovative writings, like 'The Railroad Earth' and his "try at a spontaneous *Finnegans Wake*" – *Old Angel Midnight*. Neglected writings, such as *Tristessa* and *Big Sur*, are also analysed, alongside better-known novels such as *Dharma Bums* and *Desolation Angels*.
R.J. Ellis is Senior Lecturer in English at Nottingham Trent University.
1999 • 294 pages • ISBN 978-1-871551-53-2

Musical Offering *by Yolanthe Leigh*
In a series of vivid sketches, anecdotes and reflections, Yolanthe Leigh tells the story of her growing up in the Poland of the 1930s and the Second World War. These are poignant episodes of a child's first encounters with both the enchantments and the cruelties of the world; and from a later time, stark memories of the brutality of the Nazi invasion, and the hardships of student life in Warsaw under the Occupation. But most of all this is a record of inward development; passages of remarkable intensity and simplicity describe the girl's response to religion, to music, and to her discovery of philosophy.
Yolanthe Leigh was formerly a Lecturer in Philosophy at Reading University.
2000 • 56 pages • ISBN: 978-1-871551-46-4

In Pursuit of Lewis Carroll *by Raphael Shaberman*
Sherlock Holmes and the author uncover new evidence in their investigations into the mysterious life and writing of Lewis Carroll. They examine published works by Carroll that have been overlooked by previous commentators. A newly-discovered poem, almost certainly by Carroll, is published here.
Amongst many aspects of Carroll's highly complex personality, this book explores his relationship with his parents, numerous child friends, and the formidable Mrs Liddell, mother of the immortal Alice. Raphael Shaberman was a founder member of the Lewis Carroll Society and a teacher of autistic children.
1994 • 118 pages • illustrated • ISBN 978-1-871551-13-6

Poetry in Exile: A study of the poetry of W.H. Auden, Joseph Brodsky & George Szirtes *by Michael Murphy*
"Michael Murphy discriminates the forms of exile and expatriation with the shrewdness of the cultural historian, the acuity of the literary critic, and

the subtlety of a poet alert to the ways language and poetic form embody the precise contours of experience. His accounts of Auden, Brodsky and Szirtes not only cast much new light on the work of these complex and rewarding poets, but are themselves a pleasure to read." Stan Smith, *Research Professor in Literary Studies, Nottingham Trent University.*

Michael Murphy is a poet and critic. He teaches English literature at Liverpool Hope University College.

2004 • 266 pages • ISBN 978-1-871551-76-1

Wordsworth and Coleridge: Views from the Meticulous to the Sublime
by Andrew Keanie
For a long time the received view of the collaborative relationship between Wordsworth and Coleridge has been that Wordsworth was the efficient producer of more finished poetic statements (most notably his long, autobiographical poem *The Prelude*) and Coleridge, however extraordinary he was as a thinker and a talker, left behind more intolerably diffuse and fragmented works. *Wordsworth and Coleridge: Views from the Meticulous to the Sublime* examines the issue from a number of different critical vantage points, reassessing the poets' inextricable achievements, and rediscovering their legacy.

Andrew Keanie is a lecturer at the University of Ulster. He is the author of articles on William Wordsworth, Samuel Taylor Coleridge and Hartley Coleridge. He has written three books for the Greenwich Exchange *Student Guide Literary Series* on Wordsworth, Coleridge and Byron.

2007 • 206 pages • ISBN 978-1-871551-87-7 (Hardback)

POETRY

Adam's Thoughts in Winter *by Warren Hope*
Warren Hope's poems have appeared from time to time in a number of literary periodicals, pamphlets and anthologies on both sides of the Atlantic. They appeal to lovers of poetry everywhere. His poems are brief, clear, frequently lyrical, characterised by wit, but often distinguished by tenderness. The poems gathered in this first book-length collection counter the brutalising ethos of contemporary life, speaking of, and for, the virtues of modesty, honesty and gentleness in an individual, memorable way.

2000 • 46 pages • ISBN 978-1-871551-40-2

Baudelaire: Les Fleurs du Mal *Translated by F.W. Leakey*
Selected poems from *Les Fleurs du Mal* are translated with parallel French texts and are designed to be read with pleasure by readers who have no French as well as those who are practised in the French language.

F.W. Leakey was Professor of French in the University of London. As a scholar, critic and teacher he specialised in the work of Baudelaire for 50 years and published a number of books on the poet.
2001 • 152 pages • ISBN 978-1-871551-10-5

'The Last Blackbird' and other poems by Ralph Hodgson *edited and introduced by John Harding*
Ralph Hodgson (1871-1962) was a poet and illustrator whose most influential and enduring work appeared to great acclaim just prior to, and during, the First World War. His work is imbued with a spiritual passion for the beauty of creation and the mystery of existence. This new selection brings together, for the first time in 40 years, some of the most beautiful and powerful 'hymns to life' in the English language.
John Harding lives in London. He is a freelance writer and teacher and is Ralph Hodgson's biographer.
2004 • 70 pages • ISBN 978-871551-81-5

Lines from the Stone Age *by Sean Haldane*
Reviewing Sean Haldane's 1992 volume *Desire in Belfast*, Robert Nye wrote in *The Times* that "Haldane can be sure of his place among the English poets." This place is not yet a conspicuous one, mainly because his early volumes appeared in Canada, and because he has earned his living by other means than literature. Despite this, his poems have always had their circle of readers. The 60 previously unpublished poems of *Lines from the Stone Age* – "lines of longing, terror, pride, lust and pain" – may widen this circle.
2000 • 52 pages • ISBN 978-1-871551-39-6

Lipstick *by Maggie Butt*
Lipstick is Maggie Butt's debut collection of poems and marks the entrance of a voice at once questioning and self-assured. She believes that poetry should be the tip of the stiletto which slips between the ribs directly into the heart. The poems of *Lipstick* are often deceptively simple, unafraid of focusing on such traditional themes as time, loss and love through a range of lenses and personae. Maggie Butt is capable of speaking in the voice of an 11th-century stonemason, a Himalayan villager, a 13-year-old anorexic. When writing of such everyday things as nylon sheets, jumble sales, X-rays or ginger beer, she brings to her subjects a dry humour and an acute insight. But beyond the intimate and domestic, her poems cover the world, from Mexico to Russia; they deal with war, with the resilience of women, and, most of all, with love.
Maggie Butt is head of Media and Communication at Middlesex University, London, where she has taught Creative Writing since 1990.
2007 • 72 pages • ISBN 978-1-871551-94-5

Martin Seymour-Smith – Collected Poems *edited by Peter Davies*
To the general public Martin Seymour-Smith (1928-1998) is known as a distinguished literary biographer, notably of Robert Graves, Rudyard Kipling and Thomas Hardy. To such figures as John Dover Wilson, William Empson, Stephen Spender and Anthony Burgess, he was regarded as one of the most independently-minded scholars of his generation, through his pioneering critical edition of Shakespeare's *Sonnets*, and his magisterial *Guide to Modern World Literature*.
To his fellow poets, Graves, James Reeves, C.H. Sisson and Robert Nye – he was first and foremost a poet. As this collection demonstrates, at the centre of the poems is a passionate engagement with Man, his sexuality and his personal relationships.
2006 • 182 pages • ISBN 978-1-871551-47-1

Shakespeare's Sonnets *by Martin Seymour-Smith*
Martin Seymour-Smith's outstanding achievement lies in the field of literary biography and criticism. In 1963 he produced his comprehensive edition, in the old spelling, of *Shakespeare's Sonnets* (here revised and corrected by himself and Peter Davies in 1998). With its landmark introduction and its brilliant critical commentary on each sonnet, it was praised by William Empson and John Dover Wilson. Stephen Spender said of him "I greatly admire Martin Seymour-Smith for the independence of his views and the great interest of his mind"; and both Robert Graves and Anthony Burgess described him as the leading critic of his time. His exegesis of the *Sonnets* remains unsurpassed.
2001 • 194 pages • ISBN 978-1-871551-38-9

The Rain and the Glass *by Robert Nye*
When Robert Nye's first poems were published, G.S. Fraser declared in the *Times Literary Supplement*: "Here is a proper poet, though it is hard to see how the larger literary public (greedy for flattery of their own concerns) could be brought to recognize that. But other proper poets – how many of them are left? – will recognize one of themselves."
Since then Nye has become known to a large public for his novels, especially *Falstaff* (1976), winner of the Hawthornden Prize and The Guardian Fiction Prize, and *The Late Mr Shakespeare* (1998). But his true vocation has always been poetry, and it is as a poet that he is best known to his fellow poets.
This book contains all the poems Nye has written since his *Collected Poems* of 1995, together with his own selection from that volume. An introduction, telling the story of his poetic beginnings, affirms Nye's unfashionable belief in inspiration, as well as defining that quality of unforced truth which distinguishes the best of his work: "I have spent my life trying to write

poems, but the poems gathered here came mostly when I was not."
2005 • 132 pages • ISBN 978-1-871551-41-9

Wilderness *by Martin Seymour-Smith*
This is Martin Seymour-Smith's first publication of his poetry for more than twenty years. This collection of 36 poems is a fearless account of an inner life of love, frustration, guilt, laughter and the celebration of others. He is best known to the general public as the author of the controversial and bestselling *Hardy* (1994).
1994 • 52 pages • ISBN 978-1-871551-08-2

EDUCATION

Making School Work *by Andy Buck*
Full of practical examples, this book sets out a range of strategies for successful school leadership. It provides examples of tried and tested ideas to use when tackling some of the key challenges facing every school leader: This book aims to offer readers a range of practical approaches to both policy and leadership style, based around a series of case studies and school-based policies. Each chapter examines a key challenge facing school leaders and provides practical ideas and strategies that have been shown to work in schools.
A geography teacher since 1987, Andy Bucks' experience has included working as a head of department, head of year, deputy head and two headships, all in London schools.
2007 • 142 pages • ISBN 978-1-871551-52-5

HISTORICAL FACTION

The Secret Life of Elizabeth I *by Paul Doherty*
A detective story with a difference – tracking down the real Elizabeth I – capturing the atmosphere of Elizabethan and Jacobean England, with stunning results. Paul Doherty's original research shows Elizabeth I of England to be a strongwilled, brilliant ruler but also a woman with deep passions and fervent attachments. The lady-in-waiting describes the passionate relationship between Elizabeth and Robert Dudley, later Earl of Leicester. She reveals evidence about the strange death of Dudley's wife, the very physical relationship between Elizabeth and Dudley, and the stunning revelation that they had a son, Arthur Dudley, seized by the Spanish in 1587.
Paul Doherty is an internationally renowned author. He studied history at

Liverpool and Oxford Universities, gaining his doctorate at Oxford. He is now the headmaster of a very successful London school. First in the series published by Greenwich Exchange.
2006 • 210 pages • ISBN 978-1-871551-85-3 (Hardback)

Death of the Red King *by Paul Doherty*
Was William Rufus, the Red King, accidentally killed by one of his own men while hunting or is there a more chilling interpretation of his death? Doherty demonstrates that the Red King's death is highly suspect. Walter Tirel has been cast as the villain of the piece. However, through the eyes of Anselm the great philosopher, this faction develops a quite different version of his death.
Second in the series published by Greenwich Exchange.
2006 • 190 pages • ISBN 978-1-871551-92-1 (Hardback)

BUSINESS

English Language Skills *by Vera Hughes*
If you want to be sure, (as a student, or in your business or personal life), that your written English is correct, this book is for you. Vera Hughes' aim is to help you to remember the basic rules of spelling, grammar and punctuation. 'Noun', 'verb', 'subject', 'object' and 'adjective' are the only technical terms used. The book teaches the clear, accurate English required by the business and office world. It coaches acceptable current usage and makes the rules easier to remember.
Vera Hughes was a civil servant and is a trainer and author of training manuals.
2002 • 142 pages • ISBN 978-1-871551-60-0